Essential Houseplant Mastery

The Novice's Guide to Growing &
Propagating the 12 Easiest Houseplants

RAFFAELE DI LALLO

CONTENTS

1   Pothos   1

2   ZZ Plant   6

3   Snake Plant   11

4   Parlor Palm   20

5   Cast Iron Plant   24

6   Peace Lily   27

7   Christmas Cactus   30

8   Lucky Bamboo   34

9   Air Plants   38

10   African Violet   44

11   Monstera Deliciosa   49

12   Chinese Money Plant   54

13   Watering   63

14   Fertilizing   71

15   Repotting   77

16   Humidity   85

17   Best Thing You Can Do   88

     For Your Houseplants

     Conclusion   92

     About the Author   93

1 POTHOS

STORY TIME ABOUT POTHOS

Before getting into some details about how to grow Pothos, let me tell you a story. I was once moved to an office at my workplace that had no windows. ZERO windows! Much to my dismay, I immediately knew that my choice of plants for my space was more limited.

But I knew that it was not impossible by ANY means to be able to grow a few different plants in that space! There is a plant for EVERY location!

I frequently tell people that it is all about the right plants for the right space. If you try and force a plant to grow in certain conditions that it was not meant to grow in, you will be doomed to fail. Sure, the plant might look OK for a while, but it will quickly decline. If I were to put a cactus or succulent in my windowless office, the plants would succumb to a slow miserable death. I have a friend that tried that and it didn't work too well.

So, what did I do? The first plant I brought into my windowless office was a Pothos plant. I was only in that office for about a year or so. Not only did it not have any windows, but the room was completely dark every Saturday and Sunday when I was not at work, and the door was closed. There were overhead fluorescent lights though that were on for several hours Monday through Friday. Talk about extreme conditions!

But guess what? Over the course of the year, my Pothos plant thrived and multiplied several times in size from its original size. I also brought in some clear fishing string and I started to train it against the painted cinder block wall. I became the talk of the building because I had a thriving jungle in my windowless space.

Random people that I didn't know would frequently stop by to admire my jungle that included Pothos and several other types of plants including Parlor Palm, Lucky Bamboo, and Peace Lily.

Are these conditions that I described ideal? Absolutely not, but it is definitely possible to grow Pothos, and even some other plants, in these conditions. Just don't try bringing in a cactus, succulent, or any other plant that requires a lot of direct sun or I will personally come and hunt you down...just kidding. You get the point. Right plant for the right conditions. Don't forget that.

Pothos is one of the most widespread, popular houseplants that you can grow. And you will see it everywhere! There is a very good reason for this though. Although it is very common, it is truly one of the easiest houseplants that you can grow, and is also a cinch to propagate so you'll be able to easily share with family and friends! (Or maybe you'll keep the offspring for yourself! There is nothing wrong with that...Propagation can be addicting.)

Often times, Pothos is one of the first houseplants that someone buys. And under the right conditions, Pothos is a very rapid grower so this makes it particularly satisfying, as well as confidence-building, to grow!

The botanical name for this plant is Epipremnum aureum, but most of us know it by Pothos or Devil's Ivy.

Regardless what you call it, it has many fantastic qualities and deserves to be part of ANY houseplant collection...as common as it is!

The name of the genus, Epipremnum, tells us how it grows in nature. "Epi" is Greek for upon and "premnon" means trunk. These plants climb up trees and attach themselves with aerial roots. Pothos will also ramble on the ground and serve as a ground cover. Unfortunately, it has been introduced to many tropical areas and has become invasive. Fortunately for us though, they make absolutely stunning houseplants!

GROWING POTHOS

LIGHT

In general, Pothos grow very well in bright indirect light. They do not like too much direct sun, but they are quite versatile and will tolerate quite a range of light conditions. Avoid too much strong direct sun. A Northern or Eastern exposure window works very well. Morning sun is perfectly fine and is gentle enough to grow quite a large variety of plants, including Pothos.

If you choose to grow Pothos in Western or Southern exposure windows, it may require any direct sun to be filtered so that the leaves don't burn. This is especially the case if you are growing varieties of Pothos that have a lot of variegation. Just be aware that if you have more heavily variegated varieties of Pothos, such as Marble Queen, they will not be nearly as vigorous as the "plain" old Golden Pothos.

There are very few plants that I would even consider growing away from a window. As you've seen from my windowless office story above, Pothos is one of them!

TEMPERATURE

As far as temperatures requirements, Pothos are tropical plants and do best with warm temperatures of 70F and above. Pothos is native to the Solomon Islands. The climate averages around 27C (about 81F) with little change in temperature year-round. So this is a strong indication of the conditions that you should strive to give your Pothos!

Pothos will huff and puff at you if you try growing them in a cooler room. If your room is on the chillier side, this may not be the best plant for that space. I had a Pothos once in our sunroom that sulked because it was too cool. We hadn't replaced our windows yet so the room would stay pretty chilly in the winter. I moved the Pothos out of that room into a warmer bathroom. Not surprisingly, the plant finally started to thrive.

I think many people underestimate the need for warmer temperatures when it comes to growing many houseplants. I remember one time someone was asking me for advice on growing an Alocasia amazonica (which is NOT a beginner's plant). After a series of rapid-fire questions, I came to find out that the plant was exposed to temperatures in the 40F range. Many plants are just not meant to exist in those temperatures.

WATERING

If you follow me on Instagram (@ohiotropics) and my blog,

www.ohiotropics.com, you should be quite familiar with my method and technique of watering. I will elaborate more on the general topic of watering in a later chapter in this book.

Water your Pothos thoroughly and wait until at least the surface of the soil is dry to the touch before watering again. I always water all my houseplants deeply until water comes through the drainage hole at the bottom of the pot. At the same time, you don't want to allow the soil to dry out completely.

Every time you let the soil completely dry out, the lower leaves on the Pothos vines will turn yellow and you will start to lose a lot of leaves. Conversely, never let your Pothos sit in water for extended periods of time otherwise your plant will suffer as well. This will encourage root rot and your whole plant will start to wilt, and in extreme cases, will completely die.

FERTILIZING

Most all-purpose or balanced houseplant fertilizers are good to use. See the Fertilizing chapter for further details. Like all of my houseplants, I like to fertilize dilutely at every watering starting in late Winter and continuing through early Fall.

PROPAGATING POTHOS

Pothos is one of the easiest, and quickest, houseplants to propagate. Simply take a cutting of the vine and place it in a jar or vase of water until it roots. You can even see little brownish knobs along the vine. Ensure that at least one node, where the leaf meets the stem, is under water.

You may need to snip one leaf off at the bottom of the cutting so that you are able to insert the cutting easily into the jar or vase. Be sure you don't snip off the aerial root that is often already there on the vine. These nodes are where the roots will start growing once you place them in water. In nature, these are the aerial roots that Pothos will use to attach onto tree trunks.

You can make multiple cuttings from a single vine. And don't be afraid to prune your plant! It will be rejuvenating for the parent plant and the vines will grow back.

Also, you will need to ensure that you leave at least one or two leaves on the cutting. Don't make your cuttings terribly long. A few inches long will suffice.

You can pot up the cuttings into soil when the roots are an inch or two long. Don't wait too long though otherwise your plant will become too accustomed to growing in water. Then it will have a harder time transitioning to growing in soil.

For a video illustration of this propagating process, check out my video on YouTube where I propagate an Epipremnum 'Cebu Blue' which is related to the common "Pothos."

TO HANG OR NOT TO HANG?

Pothos often times is sold in hanging baskets. I've certainly grown many Pothos this way, hanging from a ceiling hook, or displayed on top of a cabinet. And it certainly makes sense given its rapid, trailing growth.

Another more interesting way to grow Pothos is to grow it as a floor plant with a moss pole. You can then tie the vines loosely against the moss pole as it grows. By growing it this way, the plant will actually start to produce larger leaves than it would have if it didn't have a climbing support.

I converted one of my Pothos into a floor specimen and I added a moss pole which I purchased from Amazon. Just do a search online for moss posts, or you may also want to do a DIY project and make your own!

What more can you ask from a plant? As common as it is, Pothos tolerates a very wide range of light conditions, grows quickly, and is super easy to propagate. There is a reason why this plant is so enormously popular!

2 ZZ PLANT

STORY TIME ABOUT ZZ PLANT

Recently, I reconnected with a former grade school classmate through Instagram. She was well aware of my plant prowess, through my burgeoning Instagram following (@ohiotropics) and also through my blog site www.ohiotropics.com.

Her mother had run into a dilemma. Her ZZ plant had simply gotten too big and she needed to re-home the plant. My classmate would frequently show her mother my Instagram posts. I was flattered to find out that her mother chose me as the heir to the precious plant. I quickly arranged a day and time for me to pick up the plant.

As I arrived to her condo, she greeted me with a hug. I had met my classmate's mother decades ago in grade school but had not seen her since. She introduced me to a gigantic ZZ plant that was sitting behind the door in the foyer of the condo. It must have been a good 4 feet in diameter! She said that someone had given it to her a few years ago, but it has gotten too big for the space.

As far as the care for that plant, she said she would water the plant once a month, and that's it. I immediately thought, "How am I going to fit that in my car?" Before I could even think about what to do, she scooped the plant up and started carrying it to my car. As she was walking to my car, she quipped "You need to meet my neighbor. She has another plant for you too." What was I supposed to do except oblige to her request? I certainly find it very difficult to say no to anyone insisting that they want to give me their plants.

After somehow fitting the monster ZZ plant into the back seat of my car, we walked just a few steps over to her neighbor's condo and rang the doorbell. A friendly older lady opened the door with a smile on her face. We exchanged quick introductions, and before I knew it, her neighbor proceeded to scoop up a beautiful Ming Aralia and presented it to me with outstretched arms.

I was not aware of this second bonus plant, but I accepted it with gratitude with both arms. It wasn't as wide as the ZZ plant, but it was taller. Ming Aralia is definitely not a plant for beginners, but the ZZ Plant certainly is! In fact, there are few plants better than a ZZ plant for the complete beginner!

The botanical name for this plant is Zamioculcas zamifolia. Do you see why it's called ZZ plant? Much easier to say than Zamioculcas zamifolia!

GROWING ZZ PLANT

LIGHT

ZZ plant is one of those houseplants that will survive practically anywhere you will put it. Anywhere between complete darkness and direct sun will be suitable for this plant, and this is not an exaggeration.

The best-case scenario would be to have bright indirect light, and a little bit of direct sun won't hurt at all. Although this plant is tolerant of very low light, don't expect it to grow too much if your light is very poor. It is very tolerant, however, and it would be a perfect plant even for office areas with no windows and only overhead lighting.

When you see a plant tag that says "low light," it doesn't necessarily mean that the plant NEEDS low light. It simply means that it will TOLERATE low light. That being said, this plant will still look great in lower light situations, but don't expect it to grow too rapidly, and it may weaken over time. This plant is one of the best plants for lower light conditions, rivaling only a handful of others like Pothos and Sansevieria.

I have a ZZ plant on top of my kitchen table, which is a few feet away from a Western exposure window. There is also a skylight right above the kitchen table. Throughout the year, it may get a glimmer of direct sun occasionally, but most of the day it sits in indirect light. I would still consider it a lower light situation, but it is sufficient for me since the new growth is strong and the growth rate is actually much faster than I expected for this plant.

If your growth is floppy and very weak, you may need to increase your light levels. But don't go too far in the other direction as you don't want these sitting in a lot of direct sun either.

TEMPERATURE

This plant is best grown in temperature ranges of 65F-80F.

WATERING

ZZ plants will tolerate a great amount of neglect when it comes to watering. Similar to lighting conditions however, if you DON'T completely ignore the watering needs of your ZZ plant, it will reward you! But if you are a forgetful waterer, this is one of the best plants that you can grow.

Those of you that follow me on Instagram (@ohiotropics) know my stance on watering. I like to water thoroughly until water drains out of the drainage holes. For ZZ plants, I will wait quite a while before watering again. I don't really use a calendar to determine when I water because it will drastically vary depending on many factors. See the watering chapter later in this book.

After watering it thoroughly, I will wait pretty much until all of the soil is completely dry. You definitely want to at least wait until the top inch or two of the soil is dry before watering again. Don't even THINK about watering this plant again if you touch the surface of the soil and it is still moist!

Never let this plant sit in water for extended periods of time, otherwise it may quickly rot. It is very difficult to kill this plant unless you go heavy with the watering can!

FERTILIZING

Most all-purpose or balanced houseplant fertilizers are good to use. See the Fertilizing chapter for further details. Like all of my houseplants, I like to fertilize dilutely at every watering starting in late Winter and continuing through early Fall.

PROPAGATING ZZ PLANT

There are a couple ways that you can propagate the ZZ plant.

The quickest way is by division. When you repot the plant, you would simply divide the plant at the root system and then simply repot. This may be a little tricky though because the plant produces very thick rhizomes so it may not be the easiest unless you want to instantly make new plants. You may run the risk of damaging the plant however since the rhizomes can be difficult to work with.

The other method, which is the safest but takes longer, is simply to take leaf cuttings! The procedure is as follows:

• Snip a single leaf off of the plant. It is best to take a few leaves because not all of them will necessarily root!

• Allow the leaves to air dry for a day or so.

• Insert the end of each leaf, where it was cut, partially into a pot to which you've added a special potting mix. About 1/3 of the leaf or so should be in the potting mix. Enough so that it is stable and doesn't wobble around. For the potting mix, you can use about half seed starting potting mix (or even a normal all-purpose potting mix if that's what you have on hand) and half perlite. Or if you have a cactus/succulent mix, use half of this mixture and half perlite.

• Water very lightly and place the pot in a warm location with bright indirect light.

• Then just wait! Water occasionally when the potting mix gets too dry.

Depending on how warm your home is, it may root is as quickly as a month, or it could take several months. Warmer conditions will make the process go much more quickly. If you get curious, you can gently pull the leaf out after a month or so and inspect for any roots and rhizome formation. You can pot it up into its own pot after this, or leave it in the pot that you propagated it in.

3 SNAKE PLANT

STORY TIME ABOUT SANSEVIERIA

Sansevieria is probably one of the easiest, most carefree houseplants that you can grow. Sansevieria is the name of the genus, but you may know this plant by the common names of snake plant, or even mother-in-law's tongue.

Sansevieria is commonly planted in office buildings, shopping malls and other areas, because they are grown so easily and tolerate a lot of neglect!

Don't be fooled though because there are so many more varieties than the plain green ones that you see everywhere. There is actually quite a nice variety of Sansevieria, ranging from ones that grow a few inches tall, up to varieties that can grow a few feet tall!

If I were to choose ONE beginner plant, this is it. No houseplant collection is complete without at least one Sansevieria…or two…or three. Once you start growing them, you'll find that they are a delight and will probably be among the least demanding houseplants that you can grow at home. You'll find yourself addicted to growing them.

GROWING SANSEVIERIA

LIGHT

This is another one of those plants that are often labeled as "low light" plants. What does it mean if you pick up a Sansevieria and the label says Low Light? Some people mistakenly think that this means that the plant NEEDS low light. This couldn't be further from the truth. Similar to the ZZ plant, what it DOES mean is that it will TOLERATE low light.

Did you know that many Sansevierias in nature grow in plenty of direct sunshine? This is a far cry from the "low light" perception that is conveyed from reading a plant label. That being said, this plant IS in fact tolerant of low light. However, if you want a truly beautiful Sansevieria, it is best to grow them in brighter light!

As long as you place them in front of any window (whether it is North, East, West or South), it will be infinitely better than relegating a Sansevieria to a dark corner in your home. I personally have all my Sansevieria in both East and West windows. If you do expose your plant to significant amount of direct sunshine, just watch for any signs of leaf scorch and adjust as needed.

Depending on where you live, they can easily take even a half day's worth of sun. Just keep in mind that if you do have your Sansevieria in a darker location and far away from a window, it will survive. However, it will eventually decline and not do its best. The growth will be weaker and the leaves may even start to bend and lean over. These are indications that your plant is not getting the light that it needs to look its best.

TEMPERATURE

Similar to many of the plants in this book, Sansevieria grow best in warmer conditions. If you are cold, your Sansevieria will likely be cold. Try not to expose these plants to temperatures much below 50F for best results.

WATERING

Regardless of the type of plant, the way I water plants is largely the same. You may find this a little shocking.

BUT, what I do vary when watering different types of plants is the extent to which I let the soil dry out in between watering.

If you read on a label that Sanseveria is a "Low Moisture" plant, what exactly does that mean? Similar to what I previously described as far as "low light" on a label, this can be very misleading and there will be room for a lot of assumptions when it comes to interpreting a plant label. Does "low moisture" on the label mean that you should just give your plant a tiny little drink of water at every single watering? My answer to that is, absolutely not.

Many people have been shocked at how I water plants, especially Sansevieria and many different types of succulents. I will take most of my plants (assuming that they are small enough to carry), to a sink and give them a thorough soaking regardless of the type of plant!

What I DO vary however, is how dry I let the soil get in BETWEEN watering. For Sansevieria, since they naturally grow in dry soil in nature, I will let the soil completely dry out before watering again. For a fern, I wouldn't dare follow this same method. Doing so will result in a quick death for your fern! I absolutely still water ferns thoroughly, but I normally wait until the surface of the soil is just barely dry before watering again. Ferns like a consistently moist potting medium.

If I were to treat my ferns like Sansevieria and let their soil dry out completely, I would have some pretty ugly and crispy ferns on my hands. To summarize, water your plants thoroughly, but you'll need to customize your watering regime to different levels of soil dryness, depending on the plant that you have, before watering again.

It is my whole-hearted opinion that most people kill their succulents by either overwatering, or conversely, by not watering thoroughly. Don't make the mistake of not watering your plants thoroughly at each watering session. Soak the soil until water drains out through the drainage hole. Don't let your Sansevieria sit in water however for extended periods or it may rot.

If you are skimpy with watering and don't moisten all of the soil when you water, you will be encouraging a shallow root system, and will eventually dehydrate your plant and start a slow demise.

Moral of the story: Water your Sansevieria thoroughly and then let all the soil dry out completely before repeating and watering again.

One note of caution. When you water your Sansevieria, avoid getting water stuck in the rosettes of leaves. If you get water stuck between the leaves, the plant may rot (especially at cooler temperatures).

FERTILIZING

I like to fertilize all my Sansevieria from about late Winter to early Fall or so using a good fertilizer that is formulated for Cactus and Succulents. I'm currently using a Schultz cactus fertilizer that has a 2-7-7 NPK ratio. Follow the fertilize label instructions, but the particular fertilizer I use is formulated to be used at every watering.

If your plant is growing in very low light, you may want to fertilize more sparingly.

PROPAGATING SANSEVIERIA

Plant propagation is a fun and rewarding way to learn about your plants, and it also helps to increase your collection while minimizing cost! You can use it to create more plants for yourself, or to share as gifts with friends and family. Not to mention, it is really fun to do! There are so many ways to propagate houseplants, all depending on the type of plant that you have. Snake plant propagation by leaf cuttings is fun and easy to do, but it IS a test of patience!

You can propagate various types of plants by division, air layering, leaf cuttings, stem cuttings, etc. Not to mention water propagation versus soil propagation. In this section, I will focus on propagating Sansevieria with leaf cuttings in soil.

TAKING A LEAF CUTTING

The first thing you'll need to do is a choose a leaf from your Sansevieria to cut off and propagate. I have several Sansevieria plants, but I wanted to propagate one in particular. I found a beautiful specimen on a clearance rack for $5. It looked like it had suffered some abuse and had some leaves that were damaged. Right off the bat, I decided that I should cut the ugly leaves off and propagate them.

Normally for any succulent cuttings, I recommend letting the cuttings dry out for a period of time in order for the cut to callous over and dry. This prevents rotting. In the case of Sansevieria, since the leaves really aren't particularly juicy, you may be OK to skip this step. I know of many people that have skipped this step and have been successful, but I would still do it just to be safe!

CRITICAL STEPS FOR SANSEVIERIA LEAF CUTTINGS

Be sure you read this section carefully. I've included a diagram as well to visually show it since it can be confusing to explain with just words.

First choose the leaf you want to propagate and cut it off with a pair of sharp scissors. Next, you will cut that leaf into a few segments. You'll want each segment to be at least 2-3 inches long or so.

The critical part to follow is that as you cut the leaf segments, you need to keep track of the part of the leaf segment that was closest to the soil. You can NOT turn the leaf segment upside down and then insert that into the soil. It will NOT root. If you are worried that you will mix them up, cut a little notch on the corner of the leaf segment so that you know which end to insert into the soil.

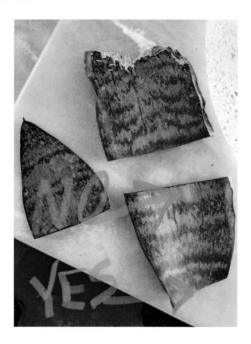

Look closely at the photo above. The area labeled "yes" is where I made the first cut on the leaf. You can not turn this segment upside down and insert it into the soil for propagation!

The same goes for all the other segments that you cut on the same leaf. The leaf segment needs to remain in the same orientation as it was originally growing on the plant. The part of the leaf segment that was originally closest to the pot will be the end that you will insert into the soil for propagation.

Notice that I also cut another leaf segment from the same leaf. Similarly, the bottom of that leaf segment will be the end that I will insert into the soil. I chose this leaf because it was ugly and damaged when I purchased the plant, so I figured I'd cut it off to improve the appearance of the original plant, and also to propagate!

PROPAGATING VARIEGATED SANSEVIERIA

Please note that if you have a variegated Sansevieria, such as the variety with a yellow stripe on the perimeter of the leaf that I have pictured in the very beginning of the chapter, the leaf cutting propagation method will NOT result in variegated plants. It will revert to the non-variegated version of the plant.

If you want to propagate a variegated variety and KEEP the variegation, you can still propagate the plant, but you can't use the leaf cutting method of propagation. You would simply need to divide the original plant at the roots and pot up each division in separate pots.

AFTER YOU HAVE CUT YOUR LEAF SEGMENTS

After you have followed the steps above, it is almost time to place them into soil.

Follow these steps:

- Dip the end of each leaf segment into water, and then into rooting hormone. You don't HAVE to use a rooting hormone, but it should speed up the process! I like to use Garden Safe Take Root Rooting Hormone, but you can use any rooting hormone. It gives great results and helps speed up the process!

- Fill a pot with soil and water thoroughly first in order to pre-moisten the soil before inserting the leaf segments into it. A succulent/cactus soil mix will work best. I really like Hoffman Organic Cactus & Succulent Soil Mix. I use it for propagation purposes and anytime I repot any cacti or succulents. In addition to this soil mix, I like to mix in a little perlite or pumice for additional porosity and drainage. I like to add perlite or pumice to all my succulent soil blends and not just for Sansevieria! You will love what it does for the drainage!

- Insert the appropriate end of each leaf segment into the soil, maybe 1/2 inch to 3/4 inches into the soil.

Now it's time to wait for Sansevieria babies to emerge! Place the pot in an area with bright indirect light. Some sun, especially morning sun, will be just fine.

Wait until the soil is almost completely dry before gently watering again.

Keep an eye out for new growth in the ensuing weeks and months. In my propagation project above, it took 7/12 months before one of the leaf cuttings produced a visible pup! I wasn't kidding earlier when I mentioned that you need to have patience! If you keep your pot in warmer conditions, it may help shorten the time that it takes for rooting and pups to appear.

WATER PROPAGATION

Another method that you can try if you don't want to do the soil propagation method I outlined above, is to water propagate Sansevieria. Water propagation can be much quicker than soil propagation for Sansevieria. Simple make the cuttings and callous them over like I described earlier, and then place them in a vase or jar with water.

Keep the bottom third or so submerged in water. If you'd like, you can also use the whole leaf instead of cutting them into segments. But if you cut them into segments, you will have the potential for more pups.

If you use the water method to propagate, you'll need to change the water frequently to keep it clean so that the leaves don't rot. I would recommend changing the water once a week at a minimum, or more if you notice that the water is dirty or cloudy.

Once your water propagated cuttings start growing roots, you can plant them in soil. Some people wait for the pups to emerge, and then plant them in soil. I would recommend planting in soil when the roots are at least a half inch or so long. The roots will typically emerge first, and then the pups will come.

The time that it takes for roots to appear in water propagation is generally much quicker than soil propagation. The fastest I've heard is rooting after two weeks. Normally, two months is pretty typical to see the first roots. However, it all depends on your conditions. Brighter and warmer conditions will help to expedite the process of rooting.

OTHER CULTURAL NOTES

Sansevieria plants need a quickly draining soil. To keep it easy, you can purchase soil blends made specifically for succulents and cacti. I really like using Hoffman Cactus & Succulent Soil Mix. To this mix, I like to add pumice or perlite to improve porosity and drainage. Or you can even add perlite or pumice to a standard houseplant potting mix that you have on hand. Miracle Gro makes a fantastic all-purpose potting mix! I use it for a variety of houseplants with great success.

Sansevieria plants like a sharply draining soil. If your soil is not well drained, you may risk root rot if the soil stays wet for too long. This will especially be the case if you have a plant growing in very low light AND you have a poorly draining soil. It a recipe for disaster. In low light, your plant will not be growing much, and therefore will use very little water. As a result, the potting mix will take a lot longer to dry out.

Growing houseplants is a balancing act and everyone's conditions are different. If someone asks me how often I water a plant, I tell them that it depends! If your plant is in a cooler and dimmer location than mine, your plant will not use up as much water and in theory will take longer for your soil to dry out. So the correct question to ask is not how often to water a specific plant, but how dry should the soil get before watering again?

4 PARLOR PALM

STORY TIME ABOUT PARLOR PALM

Each and every one of you reading this book have slightly different environments in which you grow houseplants. Different climates, different natural light, varying humidity, among other things.

I'll tell you one thing though. Where I live, the Parlor Palm (Chamaedorea elegans) is the ONLY palm that I will grow indoors! And it is not just a throw-away plant that comes in a basket of funeral plants!

For me, it is by far the easiest to grow and least problematic palm. It is popular for good reason! If you have struggled with growing palms indoors and you haven't tried the parlor palm, why don't you give it a chance? I have 3 of these in my own home.

To me, this is an ideal palm because it maintains a manageable size, grows pretty slowly and can tolerate growing in low light.

GROWING PARLOR PALM

LIGHT

I've actually grown this plant in my windowless office that I described earlier in this book. It definitely is one of the plants that can take this type of treatment! Keep in mind though, I did have overhead lighting on. No plant can grow in the dark!

Although these will tolerate very low light, you will achieve the best growth if you do give your parlor palm brighter light. I have a specimen parlor palm that I've grown for several years and it has grown into quite a nice specimen.

I have this specimen palm, pictured at the beginning of this chapter, growing in an Eastern exposure window. It receives some morning sun, and then bright indirect light for the rest of the day. This palm will not do well if it receives sun all day, but 2-4 hours or so of direct sun indoors is perfectly fine, especially if it is gentler morning sun.

I have a couple other parlor palms that I have growing in a large bathroom and they are a few feet away from an Eastern exposure window, and they also do well. This is a very versatile plant as far as growing locations indoors. Just be careful not to give them too much direct sun.

Northern exposure windows are perfect for these plants, as are Eastern windows. I would be careful with Western or Southern windows. You may want to diffuse excessive direct sun from the latter two exposure windows if applicable.

TEMPERATURE

Like most of the plants in this book, if you are comfortable in your home, then your parlor palm will be comfortable. In general, for many houseplants, be careful of going much below a minimum temperature of 55F or so.

WATERING

Palms in general require excellent drainage, so it is imperative that your parlor palm never sits in water. As I would recommend for ANY houseplant, your parlor palm pot should always have a drainage hole.

I like to let the top inch or two of my parlor palm soil, depending on the size of the pot, dry out before I water again. Then go ahead and thoroughly water the entire potting medium and let the excess drain away. Discard any excess water that collects in any trays that you may have under the pot.

At the same time, palms also hate to have their soil completely dry out, especially for extended periods of time. If you do this, you may experience dry, brown tips on the fronds, and your lower fronds may turn yellow and eventually turn completely brown.

FERTILIZING

I like to fertilize my parlor palm at a diluted strength with every watering. This is the technique that I prefer using for all my houseplants. This way I don't have to remember when I last fertilized! See the fertilization chapter near the end of this book for more details on watering and fertilizing.

I will fertilize with a good, balanced all-purpose fertilizer during the main growing season. Roughly, from February or March up until October or so. I withhold fertilizer during the darker months of the year where growth almost comes to a halt and the days are short.

PROPAGATING PARLOR PALM

Really the only way to increase your collection of parlor palms is to grow them from seed, or divide a pot that has multiple plants in it. You are not able to propagate by leaf or stem cuttings.

OTHER CULTURAL TIPS

Once your plant is mature enough, you may be rewarded with a spray of yellow flowers. My specimen parlor palm often blooms for me several times throughout the year. Although the sprays of flowers are pretty, the little yellow "balls" will often drop to the floor and cause a mess! As a result, I will let them bloom for a bit, but once I notice some of the flowers start to drop, I will simply cut off the inflorescence spray to avoid a mess on my floors.

Sometimes these plants are attacked by spider mites. Regularly cleaning your plant, either by regular misting or rinsing off in a sink or shower, will help keep these plants healthy and pest free.

I don't recommend misting for the purposes of increasing humidity because it really will do nothing for you. It can be helpful to mist your plants though if you have any that are prone to spider mites, and these can be prone to them.

On the topic of humidity, read my humidity chapter near the end of the book for more information. Palms do enjoy growing in higher humidity, but the parlor palm is very tolerant of average indoor conditions, which is why I prefer it over all other indoor palms! In general, proper watering and light is far more important that providing higher humidity for your plants in general, despite what you may read in other sources.

As far as repotting goes, refer to the repotting chapter for general repotting tips. However, keep in mind that parlor palms, like many palms, are fairly shallow rooted. Try and avoid using extra deep pots when you do repot.

Finally, I do like to use a very well-draining potting mix for parlor palm. I normally use a potting mix formulated for palms and citrus. You can also use a good quality all-purpose houseplant potting mix and add some coarse sand and either larger sized perlite, or even better, pumice. This will give you excellent drainage that parlor palms love. It's always fun to come up with your own custom mixes. I often find that I'm never happy with standard potting mixes and I'll doctor them up with coarse sand, perlite and pumice, depending on what I'm planting.

5 CAST IRON PLANT

STORY TIME ABOUT CAST IRON PLANT

This plant holds a very dear place in my heart. I'm the only person in my family to be born in the United States. Everyone else in my family was born in Italy and immigrated to the U.S. My grandmother, from my mother's side of the family, came to the U.S. in 1968. She brought with her to the U.S. a piece of a Cast Iron Plant that she took from the old church in the town where my family lived for probably hundreds of years.

At one point after I purchased my first home, my grandmother gave me a division of that original plant that she brought back from Italy. My grandmother has since passed away, but I will have her plant for as long as I live. They are very long-lived plants and easily divided. I think of her every time I see the plant!

For whatever reason, I don't see many people growing this plant, which is a shame because they are super tough, are very low-maintenance, survive low-light, and make great houseplants!

GROWING CAST IRON PLANT

LIGHT

The cast iron plant, Aspidistra elatior, is one of the lowest light houseplants that you can grow. I have mine growing several feet away from an Eastern window. It receives no direct sun. It is a slower growing plant indoors, but if you give it conditions that it likes, the growth may surprise you.

Over the summers, I started placing my plant outdoors, in complete shade, and it started putting out leaf after leaf from the rhizomes. If you have slower growing plants like this, placing them outdoors during the summer months will greatly benefit your plant and speed up the growth. See Chapter 17 in this book for tips on how to properly transition your houseplants to growing outdoors during the warm months of the year.

TEMPERATURE

This is one houseplant that will tolerate pretty cool temperatures. In fact, this plant actually grows as a perennial groundcover in growing zones that stay above freezing year-round.

Depending on the sources, I've read that these plants can tolerate as low at 45F or even lower, but I would stay in the "warm" temperature range. Just keep this minimum in mind in case you have your pot outside and you forget to bring your Aspidistra indoors! It will be one of the more forgiving houseplants with respect to temperature minimums.

WATERING

These plants are not too fussy about watering. They can survive drought-like conditions, however it will look its best if you give it enough water.

I would follow my standard houseplant watering technique that applies to the majority of what I grow. I'll allow the surface of the soil, maybe the top inch or so, to dry out. Then I water thoroughly all around the pot and drain any excess away. Like any houseplant, always grow Aspidistra in a pot with drainage holes.

FERTILIZING

During the active growing season, I fertilize with any all-purpose fertilizer from late Winter through early Fall. See the fertilizer chapter for general information on fertilization. I do prefer to fertilize all my houseplants at every watering, but using a more dilute strength.

OTHER CULTURAL TIPS

Because the leaves of this plant are so broad, they will tend to attract a lot of dust. I regularly dust mine, either by wiping the leaves down with a damp sponge or paper towel, or placing it in the shower to give it a good rinse. It is very important to make sure that you keep your plants free of dust for optimal health.

Your cast iron plant may get brown tips on the leaves. If this happens, I simply cut off the brown tips with scissors. Brown tips can be an indication that your plant has been kept too dry. It can also mean that your plant is potentially very pot bound. See the Repotting chapter for further information.

PROPAGATING CAST IRON PLANT

These plants can be easily propagated by division when you repot. When you take it out of the pot to repot it (preferably in Spring), you will see the underground rhizome that is spreading. Simply take a sterilized knife or set of pruners and sever a piece of the rhizome that has at least one leaf growing off of it, and pot up each division in its own pot.

6 PEACE LILY

STORY TIME ABOUT PEACE LILY

No houseplant collection is complete without a peace lily (Spathiphyllum). Although they are very common, there is a reason for this. They are very low maintenance, will survive very low light indoors, and they often will tell you when they need water! I don't know of any other plant that will bloom in low light like this plant can.

Remember my Pothos story where I talked about my windowless office and how well the Pothos had grown? I also had a peace lily in that same office. Peace lilies make great houseplants even in windowless areas and will often bloom for you, even in those conditions! But give them better conditions, and they will reward you even more.

GROWING PEACE LILY

LIGHT

Peace lilies prefer bright indirect light. You'll want to keep too much direct sun away from these plants because the leaves will easily burn with too much harsh sun. Morning sun, however, is gentle enough in most cases as long as it is not for too long.

If you provide your peace lily with appropriate light, it should reward you with plenty of flowers. Sometimes, you will find that they even have a slight fragrance! If flowers are not your goal though, and you are happy with the beautiful glossy leaves, you can get away with less light. Just monitor your plant and you will know if it is happy or not.

TEMPERATURE

Peace lilies like it warmer, so if you are comfortable, your peace lily is probably comfortable too! Try to stick with a temperature range of 65F-85F for best results.

WATERING

These plants definitely enjoy being on the moister side when it comes to their potting soil. If you let it dry out too much, you will quickly see the entire plant start to wilt and collapse. If you notice this, be sure to give it a very thorough watering. When this happens to mine, I take it to my kitchen sink and give it a very thorough soaking. Your peace lily will quickly recover.

That being said, try not to let it get to the point where it wilts from needing water. If you wait too long, your plant may die. And if you repeat the wilting/recovering process too much, you will weaken your plant over time.

If you find that your plant has gone bone dry and you try watering your plant and the water seems to go straight through quickly and doesn't absorb much, you'll have a little work to do. Sometimes when potting mixes get super dry, they become difficult to re-wet.

In these cases, you may need to water your pot several times in a row until you can feel that the pot is heavier and that the soil has actually absorbed water instead of just streaming through. Otherwise, if you don't do this, you may find that your plant will wilt again from the soil going dry very soon afterwards.

Another note though about your plant collapsing. If your plant has wilted and collapsed, but you feel the surface of the soil and it is moist, it probably means that your plant sat in water for too long and has suffered root rot. If you notice this, promptly discard any extra water that it is sitting in and let the soil dry out. If the plant is still salvageable, repot at this point. With very few exceptions, don't let any plant, including Peace Lily, sit in water for any extended period of time. Be extra careful if you have your plant slipped into a decorative pot with no drainage hole. It should never sit in water for extended periods of time.

FERTILIZING

Most all-purpose or balanced houseplant fertilizers are good to use. See the Fertilizing chapter for further details. Like all of my houseplants, I like to fertilize dilutely at every watering starting in late Winter and continuing through early Fall.

OTHER CULTURAL TIPS

There are several different varieties of peace lilies with varying sizes of leaves, ranging from small and narrow, to large and broad. Some varieties have pretty large leaves, and all of them will attract quite a bit of dust! For optimal health and growth of any plant, you should take care of those dusty leaves.

You can either use a damp sponge or damp paper towel to wipe any dusty leaves off. Another way, perhaps quicker, would be to place your plant in the sink or in the shower, and wash off any dusty leaves, while simultaneously give your plant a nice thorough watering!

If your plant is blooming, don't be surprised if you see a lot of white pollen on the leaves. Don't mistaken this for pests. It is simply pollen, and they produce a lot!

If your plant is in good light and is frequently in bloom, wait until the flowers are spent and turn brown, and be sure to cut them off. The flowers tend to shed a lot of pollen, so if that bothers you, you may want to cut them off. Also monitor any lower leaves that have yellowed or turned brown. You'll want to cut those off as well. Good housekeeping for your plants will help to keep them clean and free of any pests that occasionally may crop up.

PROPAGATING PEACE LILY

The best way to propagate peace lily is to simply divide the plant at the roots when it is time to repot. For repotting tips, be sure to read the Repotting chapter later in this book.

7 CHRISTMAS CACTUS

STORY TIME ABOUT CHRISTMAS CACTUS

Did you know that Christmas Cacti are often mislabeled when you purchase them? Many nurseries will label both the Christmas Cactus as well as the Thanksgiving Cactus under the common names Holiday Cactus, Christmas Cactus, and even other names! Go figure why people get confused over common names!

Although Thanksgiving Cactus and Christmas Cactus are both part of the Schlumbergera genus, they are in fact different species. Thanksgiving cactus is Schlumbergera truncata and Christmas cactus is Schlumbergera xbuckleyi.

The good part is that they really have the same growing requirements, so if you like the look of the plant, you have nothing to worry about. One thing to note, as the common names suggest, is that the Thanksgiving cactus will tend to bloom a bit earlier than the Christmas cactus.

You can easily visually tell the difference between Christmas Cactus and Thanksgiving Cactus by looking at the leaf segments. The Thanksgiving cactus will have small pointy tips on the leaves, like in the photo at the beginning of this chapter. Christmas cactus leaf segments will not have the pointy tips and the segments will be rounder. They also tend to have a more pendulous growing habit than the Thanksgiving cactus.

I've been growing houseplants since I was in grade school. My family came from Italy so the joys of gardening, both indoors and outdoors, was instilled in me at a very early age. My great aunt was notorious for swiping houseplant cuttings everywhere she went, and also traded cuttings with coworkers.

While growing up in my parent's house, I received cuttings of a Christmas cactus from my great aunt's house and used those to make a new plant. I took care of it for over 15 years while I still lived with my parents, and it grew into the largest Christmas cactus I had ever seen. It was over 2 feet wide and close to 3 feet long at its longest point. In fact, it grew so huge that part of the plant collapsed under its own weight! It remained in the same pot for quite a few years. Almost no soil was left and the pot was pretty much a solid mass of roots. It hung in front of a large sliding door, facing a Northern exposure, so it received plenty of bright indirect light. It was so huge that it remained in bloom for a solid 3-4 months! Although I can't promise you the same until your plant grows to mammoth proportions.

Schlumbergera, despite having "cactus" in the common name, actually grow in tropical rainforests and originate in Brazil. They are indeed tropical cacti, and are actually epiphytes, similar to many orchids, so they'll grow on tree trunks and tree branches instead of in soil in the ground.

GROWING SCHLUMBERGERA

LIGHT

These plants generally prefer bright indirect light, although some sun is OK as well! You'll know if they are getting a little too much sun because their leaf segments will start to turn reddish or even reddish purple when the sun exposure is extreme. If this occurs, your plant is likely getting too much sun.

A Northern window will do fine (especially if it is a larger northern window), and an Eastern window would work beautifully. A Western or Southern window would work as well as long as you can protect your plant from too much direct sun by using sheer curtains or slightly closed blinds if needed. Monitor the color of the leaf segments like I described and you'll know if the plant is getting too much sun.

Don't underestimate the importance of LIGHT in growing houseplants, especially flowering houseplants. Over the years, I've heard so many people complain about how poorly their plants are doing, when they don't even have their plant situated in front of a window! With few exceptions, most of your houseplants should always be directly in front of a window. If you expect this plant to bloom, it needs to have proper light.

TEMPERATURE

These plants are jungle cacti. So it should come as no shock that they need warmer temperatures. However, in the Fall, if you are able to give these plants nighttime temperatures in the 50F-55F range for a few weeks, this will help trigger blooming!

WATERING

Ensure that your Christmas or Thanksgiving cactus has excellent drainage and is not sitting in water for long periods of time. Since it is an epiphyte and grows on trees in nature, they demand excellent drainage.

I can't recommend a frequency to water your plant, since it depends on your individual lighting and temperature conditions. Allow the top inch or so of your Christmas cactus to dry out before watering again, but at the same time, you should avoid letting the entire pot dry out.

FERTILIZING

You can use any balanced houseplant fertilizer for your Christmas cactus. Sometimes I like to use a fertilizer that's actually made for African Violets, especially right before the blooming season, in order to encourage a better show of flowering. I'll continue to fertilize until about October or so. Then I'll refrain from fertilizing until new leaves start growing in the Spring after the flowering season is over.

GETTING YOUR PLANT TO RE-BLOOM!

This is the million-dollar question! There are two main tricks to get your Christmas cactus to rebloom in December or so (as its name implies).

The first is uninterrupted darkness at night. If you have your plant in an area where you have lamps or any other lights on at night, this will deter your plant from blooming! However, you may still achieve blooming if your nighttime temperatures are in the 50F-55F range despite the lights on at night.

This temperature differential between night and day would be hard to achieve indoors though. One solution would be the place the plant outdoors in the Fall for as long as you can so that it can be exposed to minimum nighttime temperatures in the 50-55 Fahrenheit range (approximately 10-13 Celcius).

If you don't want to move your plant outdoors, you'll have to be careful not to leave lights on at night. They need evenings of complete darkness in late summer and Fall in order to set buds, especially if you don't give them cool evenings.

It's always fun to have my readers get back to me when their Christmas and Thanksgiving cacti suddenly start blooming after I tell them what they need! You'll be surprised how quickly plants respond to proper care!

PROPAGATING CHRISTMAS CACTUS

I already mentioned the gigantic plant that I propagated from my great aunt's plant. Unfortunately, that plant did not come with me when I moved out of my parent's house many years ago. However, I was able to propagate a new plant from my grandmother's Thanksgiving cactus before she passed away.

Propagating this plant is easy. I took a few segments off my grandmother's plant, let them air dry a couple days to allow the cuts to callous over, and then placed them in a jar of water. They grew roots fairly quickly, and then I then potted them up in an ordinary all-purpose potting soil. You could also put the cuttings directly into soil as well.

There is nothing wrong with it, but I prefer to use a jar of water because you can clearly see when the roots start growing. After the roots are visible and growing actively, then I pot up the cuttings. Simply use a good quality potting soil, and adding a little extra perlite in there would always be a good idea.

8 LUCKY BAMBOO

STORY TIME ABOUT LUCKY BAMBOO

Did you know that Lucky Bamboo isn't a bamboo at all? This is part of the reason why I dislike common names because they can be very misleading in many cases! The botanical name for Lucky Bamboo is Dracaena sanderiana. It is in the same genus as the "corn plant" that you may be familiar with.

This is one of the most versatile houseplants that you can grow when it comes to location indoors. I have a few of these scattered around the house and in my office at work and they are all in low light locations. They really take a beating and can survive in nothing but plain water for many years, even in locations with barely any light. I will often place these where I want a pop of greenery, but which would be too dark for many other houseplants (except maybe Pothos…)

However, if you give it some extra pampering, it will live longer and be more beautiful.

GROWING LUCKY BAMBOO

LIGHT

These plants will do best for you if you give them bright, indirect light with not too much direct sun, if any. Too much direct sun will cause all of their leaves to turn yellowish, or even burn.

Lucky Bamboo is touted as a great low-light plant, but this simply means that it will tolerate low light conditions. Provide as much bright indirect light as possible, but keep any direct sun to a minimum, for best results. You can put Lucky Bamboo in a dark corner, and it will survive for quite some time, but will definitely do better if you actually provide brighter light.

I've had one growing in my kitchen by the sink and it has been there for 4 years. It is actually in a dark corner of the kitchen but it does receive some supplemental overhead light. I have another large floor vase with several canes growing in a dark corner of our dining room, and a couple others in darker locations. All of them are growing in just plain water.

TEMPERATURE

Lucky bamboo is best grown in warmer temperatures. Average indoor temperatures are fine. Be sure not to go below the 50-55F range for minimum temperatures.

WATERING

These plants are normally sold growing in water and pebbles. I don't know if I've ever seen these plants sold growing in soil, but it doesn't mean that you can't! In fact, they will probably grow better in soil. I've just kept mine growing in water because that's how I purchased them. For whatever reason, it became the standard to grow these in water.

The best water to use for Lucky Bamboo is either rainwater or distilled water. These plants are quite sensitive to chlorine and fluoride in tap water and the plants will eventually decline over time. The chlorine that is found in tap water will eventually cause yellowing of some of the leaves. Fluoride will eventually cause brown leaf tips.

That being said, I'm too lazy to get distilled water or use rain water, so I've had mine growing in tap water, and for many years! You will get better results though if you stick with pure rainwater or distilled water.

Just one word of caution. Be very careful never to let all the water dry out if you are growing these plants hydroponically, like they are normally sold.

Your plant will suffer very quickly! Keep an eye on the water level. It can evaporate surprisingly fast, especially in warmer and lower humidity conditions.

Every week or two, be sure to empty out all the water that your lucky bamboo is growing in and replace with fresh water.

Lastly, if you are using tap water, you may notice hard, white or yellowish mineral deposits building up at the base of the canes after a while. When I see this, I just gently scrape the hardwater minerals off with my fingernail and discard the buildup. Make sure it doesn't go back into the water that the plants are growing in.

FERTILIZING

Lucky bamboo can survive in plain water for many years, even without fertilizer! If you do want to fertilize, there are special fertilizers that are formulated specifically for lucky bamboo. Simply do a search online to purchase some if you wish.

PROPAGATING LUCKY BAMBOO

Instead of propagating, you may find that it might be worth it to you to just buy more lucky bamboo. They are usually pretty readily available in many hardware stores, grocery stores, nurseries, and other locations. If there is an Asian supermarket near you, these locations typically will have a nice variety. I've seen pots being sold which have several canes clumped and tied together as a specimen, and I've also seen them sold as individual canes as well. You can obtain them pretty inexpensively!

Simply purchasing new lucky bamboo is the easiest and quickest way to increase your collection. However, you can also take cuttings from your existing plants if you wish. Take a look at the photos below where I took one tall cane that had some yellow leaves, and I cut it up into three sections.

For one of the cane segments, I carefully peeled each leaf away from the cane, and it exposed some aerial roots. I simply placed these in water and the roots will continue to grow. After the roots grow 1-2 inches, I'll pot them up into soil. These plants should do better growing in soil versus growing in plain water.

9 AIR PLANTS

STORY TIME ABOUT AIR PLANTS

Air Plants are such a fascinating group of plants! They're immediately interesting and eye catching because they don't grow in soil. You'll see them loosely placed on top of a table in garden centers, or they are sold in decorative holders. No pots and no soil! In order to understand the basics of growing air plants, let's take a look first at where and how air plants, or Tillandsia, grow in nature.

Air plants belong to the genus Tillandsia, and within that genus, there are over 650 species!

Most Tillandsias are epiphytes which means that they grow on other plants, such as on trees or branches. They don't grow in soil in the ground like most plants that we are used to.

Their roots mainly serve the purpose of anchoring themselves to another plant. It is solely a means to attach themselves and they are NOT parasitic, nor do they derive any water or nutrients from their host plant.

Tillandsia actually belong to the Bromeliaceae (Bromeliad) family of plants. Their natural habitat can vary from rainforests, mountains and even deserts mainly throughout Central and South America.

In general, the Tillandsias with thinner leaves probably come from areas that receive quite a bit of rain. Tillandsias that have thicker leaves are most likely from regions that experience much less rain, such as Tillandsia xerographica which is one of my favorites Tillandsias. This particular one is the biggest tillandsia at the bottom of the photo in the beginning of this chapter. Since air plants purchased at a garden center are often not labeled with the species, this is helpful in directing you to on how often to water them!

GROWING AIR PLANTS

LIGHT

Light should be your number one concern when growing any plant. Tillandsias are no exception. Most air plants in nature are exposed to bright filtered light since they are epiphytic and grow on other plants or trees. They may get some sun, but it is filtered sun. In the home, what does this translate to?

Well first of all, don't even think about placing your Tillandsias in a bowl on a table that is far from any window. Actually, I did do this over the holidays one winter for my Tillandsia centerpiece that I created for a holiday dinner, but it was only for 1 day. They promptly went back to their growing location the next day.

I personally grow mine in an Eastern window. This provides some morning sun, but it is gentle enough so that the Tillandsia won't burn. Place your plants within 2 or 3 feet at the most of a window, as long as they are not touching the window. The closer the better because the intensity of the light will drastically decrease the further you are from a window.

North windows will probably work as well, provided that there are no big obstructions outdoors, such as trees. An Eastern exposure is probably better. West and South would work as well, but many Tillandsias will burn if they receive too much sun. In these cases, you may need to filter the sun with a sheer curtain or blinds. The Tillandsia xerographica that I described earlier actually would appreciate some direct sun.

TEMPERATURE

Tillandsias prefer temperatures between 50F (10C) to 90F (32C). But remember, the warmer it is and the more light they receive, the more water they will use up and need.

WATERING

Despite the name "air plant," these plants cannot survive on just the air in your home in the vast majority of cases! Tillandsias still need to be watered, but since they don't grow in soil, your method of watering these plants will be a little different than you are used to! There are 3 main methods of watering your Tillandsias.

First let me tell you what will NOT work. A light misting here and there, that does not completely wet your entire plant, will not be sufficient water. Do not do this. Instead, here are 3 methods that you can choose from to water your Tillandsias:

AIR PLANT WATERING METHODS

Method 1: My preferred method, especially for loose tillandsias, is soaking the plants in water. Take a bowl of water, fill it with tepid water, and place your Tillandsias in and let them soak for a good 15-30 minutes. I normally don't like to tell people how often to water plants, but for Tillandsias, I can say that I soak most of mine once a week. The main exception for me is my Tillandsia xerographica. Since it comes from a semi-arid ecosystem, it doesn't need as much water. I soak this one about every other week.

Method 2: Another way to water your Tillandsias is soak the plant while holding it under a running faucet until every leaf is wet. If you use this method, you'll probably need to do it a couple times per week.

Method 3: Finally, you can mist your Tillandsia until all the leaves are wet and the plant is dripping. Similar to Method 2 above, you might need to do this a couple times per week as well.

Whatever method you use, please heed this warning:

After you water your Tillandsia, it is important to gently shake off any excess water so it does not rot!

What I like to do with mine after watering is I'll take each individual plant, turn it upside down and gently shake any excess water away. Then I'll lay them on a towel to let them dry. After they are mostly dry, I'll place them back by their window.

If your Tillandsias are blooming, just be careful not to soak the flowers because you will decrease their lifespan, so you may have to make some adjustments.

FERTILIZING

It is certainly not absolutely necessary to fertilize your Tillandsias, but if you do, it will result in a healthier plant, better flower production, and also encourage pups to grow.

I use a special fertilizer formulated specifically for Bromeliads (17-8-22), and available on Amazon, called Grow More Bromeliad & Tillandsia Food. I certainly don't have a regular fertilization schedule. I'll fertilize whenever I remember or feel like it, except in the dead of winter. The fertilizer helps to keep your tillandsias vigorous and also encourages more pups to grow so you can propagate more plants!

On average, I probably fertilize about once a month or so and add the fertilizer to the water that I soak the plants in. You can follow the fertilizer instructions on frequency, or see what works best for you.

PROPAGATING AIR PLANTS

Tillandsias, like any plants in the Bromeliaceae family, will only flower once. After they flower, they will slowly decline and die. But before they die on you, they will grow pups at the base and you will have new plants! At this point, you can do one of two things:

You can leave the pups attached to the mother plant and have it grow as a clump. It may grow one or multiple pups.

Or you can carefully separate the pups from the mother Tillandsia once they are at least 1/3 to 1/2 the size of the mother, and then grow it as a single specimen. Take a look at the little Tillandsia pup growing at the base of the mother plant below.

DISPLAYING YOUR TILLANDSIAS

One of the fun parts of growing Tillandsias, since they don't grow in a pot of soil, is that you can be creative in how you display them!

You can purchase special Tillandsia holders of all sorts, or you can simply display them in a bowl or dish, or with nothing at all. I have some placed in little ceramic hands, and others I have set gently in a pot (with no soil of course...).

Some people will mount Tillandsias on driftwood, or other objects, and glue the base of the Tillandsia to the support structure. This gives it a much more natural look to mimic how they grow in nature. I actually did this myself and have a YouTube video showing exactly how I did it if you'd like to do the same! It actually made it a lot easier for me to water since I don't have to deal with several loose, individual plants!

10 AFRICAN VIOLET

STORY TIME ABOUT AFRICAN VIOLET

I still grow African Violets in my houseplant collection, but I used to be totally and utterly addicted to growing and propagating these plants. Back in middle school and high school, I even cross-pollinated my African Violets to create my own hybrids. More on this topic in the propagation section of this chapter...

Needless to say, I had more plants than I knew what to do with! African violet seeds are tiny, and they are borne in profusion. Between sowing the seeds and propagating with leaf cuttings, I ended up with an entire plant stand full of African Violets! That was definitely my crazy African Violet phase, but now I only have a handful.

A few notes about the origin of these plants. African Violets are in the genus Saintpaulia. The genus is named after Baron Walter von St Paul-Illaire, the then governor of German East Africa, who discovered them in 1892. Saintpaulia species are native to Tanzania and parts of Kenya, and unfortunately, their habitat is in danger. Saintpaulia ionantha is the species parent of most modern hybrids.

GROWING AFRICAN VIOLET

LIGHT

Like any flowering plant, light is an especially critical consideration. Flowering plants typically need more light than many plants that are grown for just their foliage. African Violets love very bright, indirect light and actually require it for vigorous growth and for good flowering.

First off, if you want these plants to bloom, they need to be grown close to a window. Don't expect great results if you situate your plant in a dark part of your home. There are plenty of plants that will survive this type of environment, but don't subject your violet to this type of treatment. You can also grow beautiful African violets under grow lights and many people have wonderful success growing them this way.

There are many ways to achieve proper lighting for good growth and blooming:

I grow all of my African Violets in Eastern exposure windows. They are all within 2 feet or so of the windows. They will receive some morning sun and these windows work very well for me.

North windows may also work, but monitor your plants. Growing up, I grew dozens of African Violets in front of a big Northern exposure window. Every window is different so what works for me, may not work for you!

If you have Western or Southern windows, especially if they are unobstructed, it can be much too strong for your plants. You'll need to use blinds or sheer curtains to diffuse the direct sun otherwise the leaves will burn. If the space is bright enough, you can also experiment with setting the plant back a little further than you normally would.

The bottom line is that if your African Violet does not receive enough light, it simply will not bloom well. No one buys these plants simply for the foliage!

Last but not least, be sure to rotate your African Violet at least weekly so that it can grow evenly. Some people recommend a 1/4 turn every week. I prefer to just turn the plant 180 degrees about once a week. If you don't rotate your plant, you will notice it will start to lean toward the window and you will spoil the beautiful flat rosette shape of a well-grown plant.

TEMPERATURE

African Violets are very tender and are definitely freeze babies!

An ideal temperature would be 65F to 75F.

Avoid any cold drafts. Temperatures in the 50F range can be detrimental for African Violets. Once I had an African Violet growing in our sunroom before we replaced our windows, so it was cooler and drafty. The plant did not do very well. Once I moved it to a warmer room with equally good light, it started thriving.

WATERING

There are two ways that many growers water their violets. Some are adamant about bottom watering, and others water from the top. I personally have so many plants that I don't care to take the time to bottom water. I want to water and be done! I personally choose to water from the top. Just take care to not add water to the inner crown of the plant in order to avoid rotting.

African violets have very fine, delicate roots. They prefer an evenly moist (not WET) soil. Ideally, I will let the surface of the soil just barely dry out before watering again. Always use tepid or slightly warm water and NEVER cold water. Cold water can shock the plant, and if cold water gets on the foliage, it can cause unsightly spotting.

Be careful not to let all of the soil completely dry out. If a plant has completely dried out, you will notice it will start to look droopy. The outer leaves will start to droop first. Every time this happens, it will weaken the plant, so take special care to provide proper moisture levels for your African Violet. Your African Violet may not bounce back quite as nicely as a peace lily once it has had this kind of treatment!

FERTILIZING

If your plant has good light, you could get away with not fertilizing. However, in order to truly have stunning violets and profuse blooming, you really must fertilize! I achieve amazing results using the Optimara African Violet fertilizer that contains an NPK ratio of 14-12-14. The growth and profusion of flowering is amazing with this fertilizer.

If you've let your plant dry out completely, I would recommend not fertilizing because it may damage the fine roots. Give the plant a good soaking, and skip the fertilizing for another time.

Lastly, I like to fertilize with every watering. Of course, if you use this method, you will need to use a more diluted strength. Read the fertilizer instructions carefully and fertilize accordingly.

OTHER CULTURAL TIPS

POTTING MIXES

I would recommend using potting mixes specifically made for African Violets. Don't use a standard houseplant potting mix because it may be a little heavy for your violets. African Violets prefer a light, porous potting medium and they normally contain a good amount of peat moss.

I sometimes make my own blended potting mixes for certain plants, but I keep it easy with my African Violets and purchase pre-packaged African Violet potting mix.

The following companies make wonderful African Violet potting mixes, so any of them will suffice: Espoma, Hoffman, and Miracle-Gro.

POTS

Regardless what type of pot you choose, remember that African Violets like to be grown in smaller containers. Avoid the use of deep pots as they prefer shallower pots.

If you tend to "overwater," you could try and grow them in terra cotta pots. However, fertilizer salts tend to build up more in terra cotta pots, and this can harm the fine roots of African Violets. Also, if the salts build up on the rim of the pot, the tender, succulent stems of the plant will be damaged over time. If you use terra cotta pots, be sure to do an occasional watering with just plain water to flush out any excess fertilizer salts.

I personally prefer either plastic or glazed ceramic pots for my violets, but it is purely personal preference.

Some people have a lot of success with self-watering pots for African Violets. I've never personally tried them myself but I plan on experimenting with it. I'm normally not a fan of self-watering pots and would not recommend them for many types of plants, but I do like them for ferns, and I plan on trying it for African Violets.

WATER

Be sure to NEVER have cold water splash onto your African Violet leaves. This will cause your leaves to spot and it will be unsightly. Also, IF you get any water on your leaves at all, any direct sun that reaches your plant can cause your leaves to burn. So be sure to gently wipe or blot off any water that gets on the leaves.

PROPAGATING AFRICAN VIOLET

There are three common ways to propagate African Violets:

African Violets will produce suckers at the base of the plant. Once they are big enough, you can gently pull them out and pot them up.

Another way to propagate is to break a leaf off with part of its petiole or "stem." You can then place the bottom part of the petiole in water, or insert it directly into soil. Don't bury more than an inch or so of the petiole in the soil. New plants will grow out of where the stem was cut. There may be multiple plants so you may need to separate them out once they are big enough. African Violets grow best if you leave them as one crown, versus multiple crowns in the same pot.

The least common way to grow these plants is from seed. It is very tedious because the seeds are very tiny, and they require light to germinate. Many years ago, I hybridized own African Violets and harvested and sowed my own seeds. It was fun to see the resulting plants and flowers! But beware! This will result in more plants that you will know what to do with. So unless you have ample space or plan to give them away, you may want to stick with the other two methods to propagate.

11 MONSTERA DELICIOSA

STORY TIME ABOUT MONSTERA DELICIOSA

There are so many common names for this plant: Swiss Cheese Plant, Mexican Breadfruit, and even Split Leaf Philodendron. Common names are enormously confusing and I always refer to this plant by its botanical name (genus + species), Monstera deliciosa.

You may be wondering about the botanical name Monstera deliciosa. The genus, Monstera, literally refers to the "monstrous" proportions that this plant takes on in the wild. The species name, deliciosa, refers to its edible fruit that it commonly produces in the wild. Indoors, you may never see this, but know that it does produce an edible fruit!

These plants hail from tropical regions in the south of Mexico and also parts of Central America and are found growing at the base of trees. They will climb and attach to tree trunks via the aerial roots that they produce.

After I was on Instagram for a while, I noticed that these plants have had a resurgence in popularity in recent times. I resisted getting one for a while, but one day I finally buckled to see what the hype was all about. In my opinion, these are one of the easiest, most dramatic plants that you can grow in your home. But beware, they can get exceptionally large so make sure that you have the proper space for them! My own plant virtually tripled in size in about one year.

GROWING MONSTERA DELICIOSA

LIGHT

As you can imagine by how this plant grows in the wild, as described above, it prefers filtered light, or bright indirect light. I grow mine in a large Eastern exposure window so it receives plenty of light, including morning sun which is gentle on the plant. It can tolerate much darker conditions, but your growth won't be as spectacular. After all, plants need light to photosynthesize!

You'll want to avoid too much direct sun however, especially the harsher afternoon sun. If you live in areas that typically have a lot of strong sun, you'll want to shield your Monstera deliciosa so that it doesn't receive too much direct sun.

TEMPERATURE

These are very tender plants and you should not expose these to low temperatures. As mentioned before, a good rule of thumb for most plants would be a minimum temperature of 55F. They prefer warmer conditions though for optimum growth.

WATERING

Monstera deliciosa is pretty forgiving when it comes to watering. Just like most plants, I like to let the top part of the soil dry out before watering again.

Depending on the size of the pot, I'll let the top inch or two completely dry out before I water again. Just use your finger to test the soil moisture. Mine is growing in a 14 inch pot, so I'll let the top 2 inches, roughly, dry out before I even think about watering.

Keep in mind that larger pots may take longer to dry out than much smaller pots, so don't water by your calendar. Use your finger as your guide! If your Monstera is in a smaller pot, let at least the top inch of the soil dry out before watering again.

Avoid extremes in watering. Never let this plant sit in water otherwise it can easily rot. On the other hand, try not and let the potting mix completely dry out if you can help it. Find a happy medium!

FERTILIZING

As far as fertilizing goes, I fertilize my Monstera deliciosa year-round except for the winter months.

I sometimes rotate and change fertilizers, but I'm currently using the Schultz All-Purpose Plant Food for most of my foliage houseplants.

I like to fertilize dilutely with every watering. That way my plants receive constant nutrients, similar to how they would grow in nature, and I don't have to remember the last time I applied fertilizer!

OTHER CULTURAL TIPS

For some general repotting tips, and to know when to repot your plant, be sure to read the Repotting chapter at the end of this book.

As I mentioned earlier, Monstera deliciosa is a climbing plant in nature, so you'll want to add some support, and the perfect time to do this is when you repot your plant! This way, you will minimize the damage to any roots. Although if you are careful, you can really add support at any time.

After you take your plant out of the pot, be sure to loosen up the root ball a bit. Only choose a pot that is 1 or 2 sizes bigger than the current pot. And always use a pot with drainage holes!

I like to cover the drainage hole with a broken pot shard. This way, sater can freely make its way out, while keeping soil in the pot.

When you repot, this is the perfect time to add a support so that your plant can start climbing! As the vines grow, you can loosely tie them to the posts.

To make the support, I simply purchased some bamboo stakes and put three of them in the pot at the time of repotting. (I also like to have extras on hand because I also use them in my garden.) Then I took some garden twine and tied the top up. It is a very stable structure, and you don't have to deal with a wobbly moss post! You can see the tee-pee structure in the photo at the beginning of this chapter.

As far as potting media for Monstera deliciosa goes, I like to use a good potting mix, such as Miracle Gro Indoor Potting Mix but I also like to mix in some #3 size perlite. Use about 1 part of the perlite to 2 parts, or even 3 parts, of the potting soil. You can use a smaller sized perlite, but I find that the addition of #3 sized perlite helps to achieve a beautifully well drained potting mix and airy soil structure that these plants love.

PROPAGATING MONSTERA DELICIOSA

Who wouldn't want more of a good thing? If you want to propagate your Monstera deliciosa, it is very easy to do. There are a couple of different ways that I will describe to propagate your Monstera deliciosa.

If you are impatient and don't want to spend too much time, you can simply just cut a vine and place it in water. Not just any old vine though. You'll want to choose a vine where you see an aerial root.

Then simply just cut below where the aerial root is and place the cutting in water. The aerial root will quickly grow in water and you'll be able to pot it up in no time at all.

The other method that you can use to propagate your Monstera deliciosa is by air layering. You'll want to air layer in the exact same spot that I described above.

The benefit of doing this is that your vine will be much less stressed (versus just cutting it completely off the plant).

You can check out my blog post on air layering houseplants where you can read exactly how to do it! You can do it exactly as described in that post except for one detail. Just wrap the sphagnum moss around an existing aerial root and skip the part about cutting into the vine like I mention in the air layering post. You also don't have to use the rooting hormone in this case.

Other than those two details, you can follow all the rest of the instructions. Once it is ready, you can simply cut the vine under where you air layered and pot up your new plant! You will know it is ready because the roots will be visible through the plastic. If you are not sure, there is no harm in gently taking the moss off a few months later to see if the root growth has occurred.

LEAF PROGRESSION

One of the most rewarding parts of growing Monstera deliciosa is watching the plant evolve from its juvenile leaves, to the more mature adult leaves. Young plants have leaves that are completely solid and that have no slits or holes.

As Monstera deliciosa ages, each consecutive new leaf should have more and more fenestrations (holes) and slits among the leaves.

12 CHINESE MONEY PLANT

STORY TIME ABOUT CHINESE MONEY PLANT

Few houseplants plants have caused such an uproar in recent times as much as Pilea peperomioides, or the Chinese Money Plant. Pilea peperomioides plants are easy to care for and prices on these plants have come down dramatically. Many people have taken advantage of the demand and were charging exorbitant prices.

I often would see some people charge $50, $60, and even more for these plants! Given the scarcity of the plant, and high cost that many growers used to charge for these plants, you would think that they perhaps would be difficult to grow, slow-growing, and hard to propagate. But this couldn't be further from the truth! Fortunately, these plants are becoming much more widespread globally and prices have come down drastically.

I would see so many people post this coveted plant on Instagram and I lusted after these plants, but I refused to pay the exorbitant prices that some growers were charging for these plants. One day when I went grocery shopping around the corner from my house, there was a large display of Pilea peperomioides in the houseplant section! I could hardly believe my eyes. And they were only $9.99! Shocked and appalled, I quickly picked up a couple plants.

GROWING CHINESE MONEY PLANT

LIGHT

Light is a hard issue in general to digest as far as growing plants go. It requires some experimentation, trial and error, and observation to see what works best for YOU!

Despite what you read on the internet on many sites, this plant can take some direct sun. I will tell you what has worked well in my experience.

The general advice you'll see on many sites is "bright indirect." The dreaded bright indirect recommendation! What exactly does that mean?

I have two Pilea peperomioides plants and both are in different areas of light exposure. I have one that receives no direct sun at all, but it is just inches away from a very large Northern exposure window. I would qualify this as "bright indirect" because the room IS pretty bright, but it does not receive any direct sun. It is growing beautifully!

I have another Pilea peperomioides plant that is sitting on top of my piano right in front of a large Eastern exposure window. As a result of this, it does get some morning sun which is wonderful! I found that this plant is growing faster and bigger than the one I have in the Northern exposure window. Both are perfectly acceptable locations!

What should you avoid when it comes to light? I don't care where you place this plant, but just don't place it far away from a window! You will be disappointed and the plant will just not give you good growth.

On the opposite end, take care not to place this plant in too much direct sun otherwise you may see issues as well. A few hours of morning sun are acceptable in most cases. If you do have a very sunny window, like a sunny Southern exposure window, you may need to place it a little further back. Just experiment and monitor your plant. If it looks good and is growing well, then you know it is happy!

One last comment for light is that you need to rotate your plant every so often so that it grows evenly. You will notice that plants will start to reach toward the window. Simply turn the pot 180 degrees about once a week or so in order to keep your plant growing evenly.

TEMPERATURE

I find that these plants grow better when kept on the warmer end indoors. Try to avoid sharp temperature swing and cold drafts as these plants seem to be sensitive to that.

WATERING

Those of you that follow me closely on Instagram (@ohiotropics) know my philosophy on watering. Water thoroughly until water comes out of the drainage hole. Don't stop adding water until this happens. Let it all drain out, and then return it to its window.

I like to take my Pilea peperomioides straight to the sink and I water them there. I circle the watering can or faucet attachment all around the pot to ensure that ALL the soil will be moistened. Let ALL the water drain away. Pilea peperomioides, like all Pilea species, are very sensitive to improper watering.

As a rule of thumb, I always wait until at least the surface of the soil is completely dry before I water this plant again. Don't even think about watering if the surface of the potting mix is still moist.

FERTILIZING

As far as fertilizing goes, I like to fertilize all my houseplants pretty much year round except for the dead of winter when almost nothing is growing.

As with all my foliage houseplants, I like to use Schultz All Purpose 10-15-10 fertilizer. There are instructions on the label on how to dilute it so that you can use it every time you water your houseplants. This is how I prefer to fertilize because I can do it every time and not have the remember the last time I fertilized.

OTHER CULTURAL TIPS

POTTING MIX

This is an important section and I have a lot to say about potting mixes.

First off, these plants hate to stay wet for too long, so it is imperative that you provide the appropriate potting mix. The potting mix should be very well drained and porous. Allow me to recommend some potting mixes that work well. I purchase everything I need most of the time on Amazon to keep it simple, or visit your local nursery.

Hoffman Cactus & Succulent potting mix works very well. Just because it is labeled a cactus and succulent mix, doesn't mean that you can only use it for cacti and succulents! Your plants can't read the label after all! I achieve great results by growing Pilea peperomioides in a cactus/succulent mix.

Another blend that I like using is Miracle Gro Cactus Palm & Citrus potting mix. Both blends work wonderfully. I use these blends for most of my succulents and also for some other plants such as all my Pilea and Peperomia species, and other plants that require great drainage and the need to dry out quickly.

Sometimes if I run out of a premixed cactus/succulent potting mix, I will use any good houseplant potting soil that I have on hand, but I will amend it to make it more quickly draining.

I will use any of the potting mixes described above, but will also amend the potting mix to make it more suitable for Pilea peperomioides:

Coarse sand is wonderful to add to a standard houseplant potting soil and make it instantly suitable for succulents and plants like Pilea. You can't use any old sand though! Definitely not beach sand or finer sand because this can cause the soil to compact too much.

Pumice is a wonderful soil additive and really works well to create the aeration and porosity that many plants love. It is a great potting mix amendment for cactus, succulents, Pilea and others.

Perlite accomplishes the same as pumice, but since it is much lighter, it will sometimes float to the top when you water.

Depending on what I have on hand, I will vary what I add to my potting mix. The end goal for Pilea peperomioides is a potting mix that drains quickly and also dries out pretty quickly. So experiment with your potting mixes and see what works best for you!

One last note about potting mixes, whether I use a cactus/succulent mix, or an all-purpose potting mix, I will always add a little coarse sand and either pumice or perlite to make my Pilea potting mix.

POTS

This is really a matter of preference. You can successfully grow Pilea peperomioides in a variety of different types of pots, as long as the pot is appropriately size and not too large. If you have a pot that is too large, the potting mix may take too long to dry out and cause you problems! Especially if you also use a poor quality potting mix.

Whenever you repot your plants, a rule of thumb is only to repot into the next 1 or 2 sizes up from where you currently are. For example, if you are using a 4 inch pot and need to repot, only move up to either a 5 or 6 inch pot. No bigger! And be careful of pots that are unusually deep. These can be problematic in terms of the soil drying out quickly enough.

As far as pot construction for Pilea peperomioides, I really like terra cotta pots! They allow the potting mix to dry out sooner. Of course, this means that the soil might dry out TOO quickly! It all depends on your watering habits.

Other types of pots would work well too. Whether you choose plastic pots, glazed ceramic pots, or anything else, the important part is that the pots have drainage holes. Absolutely by no means should you plant directly into a pot with no drainage hole. However, it is OK to plant in a plastic pot with drainage holes and then slip it into a decorative pot with no drainage hole. Just slip the plant out to water it, and then return it back into the decorative pot. The plant should never sit in standing water or it will suffer root rot...and BYE BYE PILEA PEPEROMIOIDES! As I mentioned earlier, these plants are very sensitive to staying wet for too long. They are also sensitive to extreme dryness.

Speaking of pots...you will need a lot of pots! These plants are very prolific and will produce many new plants that you can share with family and friends! This takes us to the next topic of propagation.

PROPAGATING CHINESE MONEY PLANT

One of the best parts of growing this plant is that it is super prolific in producing babies! All you need is one of these plants and your home will soon be overrun with Pilea peperomioides in every room! Or you can share and give them to family and friends.

And there is nothing wrong with NOT separating the babies. You can leave them all in the same pot and this will just result in a very full plant. Some people like that look and it is certainly OK to do so! But you can easily separate the babies and pot them up into small pots and share with friends! Let's go over how to do this.

This is one of the easiest plants to propagate because perfect little plants will grow right out of the potting mix at the base of the plant. Once they have at least 3 or 4 small leaves, you can simply separate them.

Be sure to get at least part of the stem that is under the soil. If you can do this without taking the plant out of its pot, go ahead and do so. If not, it is OK to take the plant out of its pot so that you can easily separate the babies. You can use your fingers, scissors or a knife to sever the small plants.

Then simply take the little pups that you separated, and place each one in a small glass or vase of water and allow it to root. Just make sure that the water level submerges just the roots and not the whole plant.

After it has developed a few roots, you can pot it up! I would suggest 2-3 inch pots for the babies and wait until they are big enough before transplanting into a larger pot. Be careful though because those tiny pots can potentially dry out much more quickly than you'd expect.

PILEA PEPEROMIOIDES TROUBLESHOOTING

I've included a special question and answer guide below detailing common issues that people have with these plants. This IS an easy plant to grow, but if you don't know what it likes, it can give you some problems. Take a look at some of the main problems that people have had with this plant, as well as my recommended solutions.

Question: Why is my plant not growing? I've had it a while and there has been no new growth!

> **Answer**: You are probably not giving it enough light! Plants need light to photosynthesize so that they can make their own food in order to grow. You can't expect a plant to grow well if you shove it in a dark corner of your home, or if it is very far away from a window.

Question: I've heard that these plants produce a lot of babies. Why is mine not growing any babies???

> **Answer**: Nature teaches us patience. Just give it some time! If

your plant appears healthy and is growing well and receiving proper light, it is just a matter of time before it grows little baby plants. Depending on how old your plant is, it may be at least a few months before you see babies start to appear.

Question: Why are my leaves curling?

> **Answer**: There can be a variety of reasons why this happens, but one reason that this will happen is if your potting media is not drying out quickly enough. Once, I repotted one of my Pilea peperomioides into a pot that I knew was MUCH too big, but I didn't have anything smaller and was too lazy to go get an appropriately sized pot. Needless to say, the potting mix was not drying out and the newer leaves were curled. I immediately corrected the issue and replanted it into a smaller pot, and it resolved the issue. If you have a potting mix that is not well drained, this can also be an issue. Be sure to follow the recommendations on soil blends found earlier in this chapter.

Question: Why are there whitish spots symmetrically scattered on the leaves?

> **Answer**: Pilea peperomioides have pores on the undersides of the leaves and sometimes the plant will release excess minerals through these pores. It will almost look like little grains of salt. It does not harm the plant, and you can simply brush them off gently with your finger. If you switch to purified or distilled water, this issue will be eliminated. Again, it will not harm the plant.

Question: My plant is drying up so quickly! Much more quickly than it used to. Am I doing something wrong?

> **Answer**: Your plant may need to be repotted into a larger pot. This happened to me as well with one of my plants. It seemed to dry out twice as quickly as it used to, but nothing else changed (light, season, etc.) It turned out that it was very potbound, so repotting it into a larger pot did the trick.

Question: I got a yellow leaf! What am I doing wrong! Am I killing my plant?

> **Answer**: I get this complaint a lot from so many people freaking out over one or two leaves yellowing. There is no reason to worry

if the leaves were older leaves from the base of the plant. This is a natural cycle of nature! Eventually the older leaves will turn yellow. It doesn't necessarily signal that you are doing something wrong.

Question: Why are all my leaves yellowing?

> **Answer**: There are various reasons why this can occur. If more leaves that just one or two at the base are yellowing, it could be the sign of a more serious problem. "Overwatering "is one reason that you can get many yellow leaves. The potting mix needs to dry out in between watering. I actually despise the word overwatering, so refer to my watering chapter later in this book for my take on this word. It is a very deceiving word and has caused a lot of misunderstanding in plant care. Also, if you let your plant sit in a saucer of water for extended periods of time, this is very problematic.

Another reason for yellowing leaves can be lack of nutrients. Do you fertilize? If you have gone way too long without fertilizing, this can also be an issue, especially if the plant has been in the same pot for a very long time.

Finally, Pileas peperomioides that are in too much direct sun may also turn a yellow-ish green color. Simply move it to an area with less direct sun and it may correct the problem.

Question: My whole plant is drooping! What happened?

> **Answer**: When I get too busy with life and don't pay attention to my plants, this can happen. It can simply mean that your plant has completely dried out and is starting to wilt from stress. Check the soil with your finger. Does it feel bone dry? Lift the plant up with your hands. Does it feel lighter than normal? Chances are you just need to give it a good drink of water. When your potting mix gets bone dry, you may need to drench the soil a few times in order to ensure that you are thoroughly moistening the soil. When this happens, the water will seem to go straight through and not moisten the soil much. Sometimes potting mixes that have gone too dry (especially peat-based mixes), will be difficult to re-wet so water it a few times in a row until the soil is thoroughly moistened.

Your plant can also be drooping if your potting mix is staying moist for too long. You may have kept your plant wet for too long and may have started to experience root rot.

13 WATERING

This chapter contains general information that I have learned over the years to help you with the critical topics of watering and fertilizing. Besides proper light, proper watering is an extremely critical aspect of having a healthy houseplant! In order to expand your horizons, I have some references in the remaining chapters to plants that haven't been featured in this book. After all, you'll need to know what you should be growing next, right?

HOW TO WATER POTTED PLANTS

People are generally very confused over how to water houseplants properly. The problem is that it is easy to misinterpret a lot of aspects about houseplant care in general. But I attribute that to many sources not really taking the time to give a complete picture of the main factors in houseplant care. What does high light mean? What does low light mean? What does it mean if a plant likes to stay moist or dry?

This chapter focuses on one aspect of houseplant care, and that is to help you understand everything about watering your houseplant properly. Here are a few watering myths that I've come across that I would like to debunk.

MYTH #1: I shouldn't soak my succulents. They only need a little bit of water at a time.

WRONG! Almost without exception, I recommend thoroughly soaking your houseplant, regardless of whether it is a succulent or not. And no I'm not crazy. It works and I speak from experience, so trust me! Keep reading though...because you might be wondering "oh I thought succulents don't like much water?" Well that's only partially true. Let me explain because the devil is in the details.

If you just add a little bit of water, you are doing a big disservice to your plant. If you don't thoroughly soak your plant and just add a little bit of water, you are encouraging a shallow root system and/or will have dry pockets of soil. The roots that stay dry for extended periods of time will eventually shrivel up and die and your whole plant will suffer as a result. Without a healthy root system, you will not have a healthy plant.

The way that you water any plant should be the same! And the answer is you water it thoroughly! The critical part for succulents is that after you water, you should wait long enough for the potting mix to pretty much go completely dry before watering again. And when you do water again, soak it again! Let the water drain through the drainage hole and discard any extra water. Less frequent, but thorough-watering, is much superior to frequent mini-drinks of water.

MYTH #2: Houseplants Need to Be Watered Once a Week

WRONG! Well, the real answer is that it depends! In some cases, yes this may work! But only under certain combinations of conditions. It's ok to have a regular checkpoint to see if your houseplants need water or not, but you shouldn't blindly water a houseplant just because your schedule tells you to. If you watered a plant, and a week later the top of the soil is still moist, you should NOT water it again. Doing so may invite root-rot. When a plant stays too wet, you are depriving the roots of oxygen and they will proceed to rot.

As a general rule of thumb, you should wait to water until the top inch or two of the soil is dry (depending on the size of the pot). Then go ahead and give it a good soaking. There are some exceptions though. Some plants, such as succulents or cacti, should be allowed to go completely dry, or almost completely dry, before watering again...but don't wait TOO long! For ferns, I would water again when the surface is just barely dry.

MYTH #3: You Water Orchids with Ice

NO! Just...NO! Unless you've seen a monkey with a popsicle in the jungle, then you should not water your orchids with ice. This is one of the worst marketing gimmicks I've ever seen. Do NOT use ice to water your orchids. First of all, when the ice melts, it does not provide enough water in order to soak the potting medium and thoroughly moisten all the orchid roots.

Secondly, the ice can damage the roots if they come into direct contact with the ice. It makes absolutely zero sense to water orchids with ice. This scheme is mainly marketed for Phalaenopsis or moth orchids, but I have also seen it for other plants as well. Phalaenopsis come from the tropics of southeast Asia and I guarantee you they've never met an ice cube.

I almost included Phalaenopsis in this book, but the first book that I wrote is on the topic of growing Phalaenopsis! If you have been confounded by Phalaenopsis, or Moth Orchids, check out my book Moth Orchid Mastery: The Novice's Guide to Mastering Moth Orchid Culture in Less Than One Hour. I promise you there are very easy to grow if you read my book! I've taught countless people and it is a short read available in an eBook or paperback format. Or if you prefer an audio book, I have that format as well.

MYTH #4: If I Fuss Over My Houseplants, They'll Grow Better

Don't get too happy with that watering can! You have to let nature take its course and a lot of people tend to "overwater " their houseplants. Like I mentioned, it's OK to have a regular checkpoint to see if your plants need water, but don't water just because you told yourself you need to water every Saturday.

I can't emphasize the following point enough: If your calendar is telling you that it's your normal watering time, and you feel the surface of the soil and it is still moist, then don't water! On the other hand, you might find a houseplant that dried out terribly and once a week may not be enough. You may need a couple checkpoints during the week. Why is this? Watering needs vary drastically depending on:

- Temperature: Higher temperatures means that soil will dry out more quickly.

- Pot Size: Smaller pots will dry out much more quickly.

- Pot Material: Terra cotta pots will dry out very quickly because they are porous. Plastic or glazed ceramic pots will take longer to dry out. Choosing a pot type based off of your specific plant can work to your advantage or disadvantage, so choose carefully depending on the moisture needs of your plant.

- Growing Season: Depending on where you live, plants will slow down or stop growing in the middle of a dark/cold winter. They will not use as much water and you have to be careful with your plant's moisture needs especially during this time. On the other hand, during the growing season, plants will need more water.

- Root System Size: Recently I was shocked because I had watered my large hibiscus tree indoors in the middle of winter, and 3-4 days later, it was very dry. This plant has an extensive root system and is in a large pot. I probably won't be repotting that plant anymore otherwise it'll be too difficult to move. Having a pot-bound plant, coupled with increasing growth as days are getting longer, all increase the need for watering.

- Humidity: In a more humid atmosphere, soil will generally take longer to dry.

- Light Levels: The higher the light levels, the more water a plant will use. A plant that is sitting in a dark corner will use much less water than a plant that is in brighter light that is actively photosynthesizing and growing.

MYTH #5: Everything on the Internet is True

WRONG! This one is a BIG WRONG. You can tell the websites that just regurgitate material versus those that truly have knowledge to back it up. Be wary of any old website when getting houseplant care information especially when it seems vague and generalized.

I've seen so much misinformation online. So if you are researching online, trust reputable sources such as my blog, https://www.ohiotropics.com! Or if you have very specific questions, it is best to refer to the numerous plant societies out there such as the American Orchid Society, the African Violet Society of America, and any of the numerous plant societies. There seems to be one for each type of plant!

OVERWATERING HOUSEPLANTS & HOW TO WATER A HOUSEPLANT

What exactly does it mean when you hear that you are overwatering a plant? What actually happens to the plant when you overwater? This is a VERY misunderstood topic. You will also learn about signs of underwatering plants as well as signs of overwatering plants. I actually hate the term overwatering, so I will give you my take on what it means to most people, but also what it means to me! I believe the term "overwatering" is a very dangerous term and I will aim to demystify the topic once and for all.

First let's get into some symptoms of both underwatering and overwatering your houseplants. It can be a confusing topic because the signs can be the same! So you'll need to look at a more complete picture, rather than make your conclusions off of just one observation.

SIGNS OF UNDERWATERED HOUSEPLANTS

There are many different indications that you can look for that will tell you if you are underwatering your houseplant.

One indication of underwatering is that the lower leaves of your plant will turn yellow. In more extreme cases, if the plant continues to be very dry, the entire plant will wilt and collapse. For anyone that has a peace lily (Spathiphyllum), you'll know that it will quickly tell you that it needs a drink of water! Give it a good drink of water, drain the excess away, and your plant will recover quickly.

If you notice that your plant has wilted, but the soil is still moist and you haven't watered it in a while, then clearly underwatering is not your issue. In this case, your plant has likely suffered from root rot.

Underwatered plants can also have edges or tips of leaves that have turned brown and are crispy. Crispy and brown edges can also be due to other things such as over-fertilizing, and could also mean that your plant is very pot-bound and needs to be repotted.

You can also get brown, crispy leaf tips if your watering practices are not up to par. If you are not watering your houseplant thoroughly, the plant will use up all the water that it can, and when there is no water left to travel to the tips of the leaves, they will not have the moisture they need, and the tips will turn brown.

If you are not thoroughly watering the potting mix of your houseplant until the water drains out of the drainage hole in your pot, it may result in dry pockets of soil. Assuming that your houseplant has the correct combination of light, potting mix type, and has well-drained soil, you should always be watering thoroughly and completely moistening the potting mix.

If you are doing what I described above, and you are still getting dry tips, it could be that your houseplant is very pot-bound and thus not able to use water as well as it should be. In that case, you should repot your plant. Refer to the repotting chapter for more details.

Once a plant leaf turns brown, there is nothing that you can do except simply cut off the brown areas. It will never turn green again. What you can do though is to remedy your cultural practices to prevent further damage to your plant.

HOW TO REVIVE A PLANT THAT HAS DRIED OUT

If your houseplant has dried out severely, one thing you will probably notice is that when you do water it, the water will very quickly start to rush out of the drainage hole and will not seem to moisten the potting mix much. You may also see that the soil has pulled away from the perimeter of the pot. Potting soil that has dried out severely may take a little work to moisten it up again, depending on the composition of the potting mix.

If you can move your plant to a sink, move it there and water it repeatedly until you are sure that the soil is thoroughly moistened. It may take several times in order to accomplish this, but it is very important! If you don't do this, your plant may suffer severe harm and even die.

SIGNS OF OVERWATERED HOUSEPLANTS

There are many signs that you are overwatering your houseplant. In severe cases, one of the leading indicators is that your plant will be wilted despite the soil being moist. This means that your plant has gotten to the point where the roots have rotted and the plant is starting to wilt as a result.

Another indication can be brown leaves, which you will also get if your plant is too dry. However, the difference is that your leaves will be limp and mushy, instead of dry and crispy, if you have overwatered.

Other indications that you have overwatered are the following: yellowing and dropping leaves, including newer leaves and not just the old ones.

Stunted growth can also be a result of overwatering, especially when it is found in combination with the above symptoms.

Do you have mushrooms growing on your soil? This is a very good indication that your soil is staying too wet! Otherwise the fungi will not be able to survive and grow.

Finally, if you take your plant out of its pot and you notice mushy roots, and even a sour, rancid odor, this means that your roots have rotted from staying wet for too long.

SAVING AN OVERWATERED PLANT

First of all, you should NOT fertilize a plant that has been overwatered! A plant that is in stress should never be fertilized. You will actually make the situation worse.

If your plant has drastic symptoms of "overwatering", such as the whole plant wilting despite the soil being moist, I would recommend taking the plant out of its pot immediately and repotting it. Remove as much of the old soil that you can, and trim away any rotted or mushy roots. Then repot in a new pot. You will probably find that you'll be placing your plant in a smaller pot that it was originally in. That's ok! Let the size of the root system dictate your pot size.

If you place your pot in a much larger pot that it should be in, the potting mix will take a much longer time to dry out. Exactly what you are trying to avoid!

HOW TO WATER PLANTS AND HOW NOT TO OVERWATER

This all comes down to proper houseplant culture! So how can you make sure that your plant is not overwatered?

First of all, I encourage everyone to thoroughly water your houseplants. Water until all of the soil is thoroughly moistened and running out of the drainage hole. Then discard any extra water. All this is very critical in order to have a healthy houseplant!

Overwatering a houseplant does NOT necessarily mean that you are adding too much water at a single watering! The goal is to thoroughly moisten the soil and ensure that any excess is drained away. This is the proper way to water. But if some other fundamental conditions are not met, your plant will suffer.

What are these fundamental conditions that I'm referring to?

Make sure your plant has the correct light! If you shove your houseplant in a dark corner of the house, it will minimize growth, and therefore the plant will not be able to use water up like it should. The soil can potentially stay wet for a very long time. Ensuring that your plant is situated in appropriate light (meaning very close to a window!) is critical.

Potting mixes are crucial too! Use a well-draining potting soil. You really get what you pay for when it comes to potting mixes. I personally love using Miracle-Gro potting soils. Even for succulents, I like the Miracle Gro Cactus, Palm and Citrus mix. Espoma makes wonderful potting mixes too.

Even though I buy these pre-packaged mixes, I still like to mix in a good amount of either perlite or pumice. Adding perlite and/or pumice will aerate your soil, increase porosity, and create much faster drainage. I use both perlite and pumice for different cases. I tend to add some additional perlite to any potting mix for tropicals, and I tend to use pumice for succulents. Either one will do the job though. I don't have a specific ratio, but you can start with one part perlite or pumice to 3 parts potting soil. Experiment and make your own special blend!

The bottom line is that you want your soil to dry out to some extent between watering. By ensuring that your plant is receiving proper light, has a well-draining potting mix, and an appropriately sized pot, you should be good to go! These ideal conditions, in combination with proper watering, is the "secret" to making your houseplants thrive.

14 FERTILIZING

How do you know what fertilizer to use? What strength? How often should you fertilize? What do the numbers mean on the fertilizer label?

After reading this chapter, you should feel more empowered with basic fertilizer knowledge and know how and when to properly fertilize your houseplants.

WHY YOU SHOULD FERTILIZE HOUSEPLANTS

In nature, plants constantly replenish their nutrients from decaying organic matter. As leaves, branches, animal life, and other organic matter decompose, they'll slowly release and recycle their nutrients into the soil and make it available for plant growth.

In your houseplant pots, the soil can be quickly depleted of any nutrients rather quickly and it will be your job to take over by fertilizing. Most houseplant potting mixes are soilless mixes so they intrinsically have little to no nutrient levels. Some potting mixes have added fertilizer that will support plant growth for a few months.

Fertilizing and soil chemistry is a very complicated topic, but this chapter will cover very basic knowledge that will be helpful for you and your houseplants.

BASIC FERTILIZER INFORMATION

When you look at a fertilizer label, you will see 3 numbers. For example, 10-10-10. These represent the 3 primary nutrients that plants need to grow.

Soil nutrients are classified based off of the amount that they are needed by plants. The following list shows the most important plant nutrients in decreasing order of usage by plants:

Primary nutrients are needed in the largest quantity and these are: Nitrogen (N), Phosphorus (P) and Potassium (K). The 3 numbers on every fertilizer label is called the NPK ratio where N, P, and K represent the chemical symbols for those elements.

Secondary nutrients are needed in smaller amounts, but are still important. These include Sulfur (S), Calcium (Ca), and Magnesium (Mg).

Micronutrients are only needed in very small amounts, but they are still very important. Micronutrients include Zinc (Zn), Iron (Fe), Copper (Cu), Manganese (Mn), Boron (B), Molybdenum (Mo), Chlorine (Cl).

In very simplistic terms, here is an explanation of NPK:

Nitrogen (chemical symbol N) is needed for growth of leaves.

Phosphorus (chemical symbol P) is important for flower and root development.

Potassium (chemical symbol K) helps to bolster disease resistance, cold tolerance and protection against drought.

When you see a fertilizer label, for example with 10-15-10, this is telling you the NPK ratio. This tells you that the fertilizer container 10% Nitrogen, 15% Phosphorus (expressed as phosphate), and 10% Potassium (expressed as potash), respectively.

WHEN TO FERTILIZE YOUR HOUSEPLANTS

In general, you should only fertilize your houseplants when they are in active growth.

In my climate, most of my houseplants are in active growth from approximately late February through September or October.

During the dismal winter months, with short days and reduced light, I stop fertilizing. The only exception I make are for moth orchids if they are growing a flower spike.

WHEN NOT TO FERTILIZE YOUR HOUSEPLANTS

Fertilizing is not a fix for poor cultural conditions! If you have a plant in poor light that is not growing, your focus should not be fertilizer. You should first position your plant in a brighter area. Light is paramount for growth! First fix your plant's lighting conditions, and then when it starts to grow, you can further support the growth by fertilizing.

In the same way, if you have a plant that is not flowering at all, don't think that adding a fertilizer high in phosphorus will help you. Fertilizer will not cause your plant to bloom. Ensuring the proper light for your plant WILL! The fertilizer will simply increase the size and amount of your flowers. When you have the combination of appropriate light along with an appropriate fertilizing, then you are winning!

Do not fertilize your houseplant if it is in a period where it is not growing. Most of my houseplant growth pretty much comes to a halt in the winter months, so I completely cut out fertilizing when light levels are low.

If your plant's potting mix has gone completely dry, don't apply fertilizer, especially if it's at full strength. You may burn the plant roots. A good idea would be to first moisten the soil with plain water first, and then come back and fertilize at a later time.

FERTILIZING WITH EVERY WATERING

This is my preferred method to fertilize houseplants. You could fertilize at full strength at whatever frequency the fertilizer label recommends, but I prefer to fertilize with every watering at a diluted strength. Why?

Number 1 reason...I don't have to remember when I last fertilized since I'm doing it every time!

There is also a much lower risk of burning your plant.

It is a much more natural way for a plant to receive nutrients. In nature, plants receive nutrients slowly from decomposing organic matter.

Many fertilizers are designed to be used at every watering. If you have one of these fertilizers, simply follow the directions!

If you have a fertilizer label that says to dissolve a teaspoon per gallon per month, I would recommend reducing it to one fourth and use that every time you water. So add 1/4 of the amount. Or if the fertilizer label says to add a certain amount and use it every 10-14 days, reduce that quantity in half to use for every watering.

Every so often, I would recommend watering your plant with just plain water, even during the growing season. This will help flush out any excess fertilizer salts that may be building up in your pot. Terra cotta pots are notorious for fertilizer salt build up since they are so porous.

Also, you may see some crusty buildup on the surface of your soil, or along the inside perimeter of the pot. This indicates excess fertilizer salts. Flushing with clear water every so often, once every month or every few weeks, will help with this issue.

TYPES OF HOUSEPLANT FERTILIZERS

I have several recommendations of fertilizers in this section and have used all of them with great results.

I'm currently using a Schultz All Purpose houseplant fertilizer that is 10-15-10. Some fertilizers are more balanced in their NPK ratio and might be 10-10-10 or 20-20-20. Plants can't read labels. Experiment with different fertilizers and see which one works best for you. I use this all-purpose fertilizer for most of my indoor plants.

There are some specialty fertilizers which you may choose to branch off into once you get comfortable with fertilizing. Here are some of the ones that I use:

For my moth orchids, I use the Grow More 20-20-20 formulated especially for Phalaenopsis orchids. If you are interested in being able to grow moth orchids (even if you were a previous orchid killer), check out my book Moth Orchid Mastery!

For my air plants (Tillandsia genus) and bromeliads, I use the Grow More 17-8-22 fertilizer which has produced amazing results for me!

For cacti and succulents, I like the Schultz 2-7-7 formulation.

My African Violets respond very well to the Optimara 14-12-14 fertilizer made specifically for these plants. They absolutely thrive on this and the growth and flowering has been out of control!

If you have any edible plants that you are growing indoors, or even outdoors during the warm weather, I like to use only organic products. For citrus plants and any vegetables, I really love using the following products:

Neptune's Harvest Fish & Seaweed Fertilizer 2-3-1 is amazing to use regularly on any vegetable plants and also on citrus. My lemon, orange and lime potted plants love this stuff!

Morbloom 0-10-10 is a great fertilizer that I use every summer on all of my potted flowering plants outdoors. It is made from fish emulsion but does not have any odor to it, which is a plus! Actually, on my citrus plants, I use a combination of this fertilizer and the Neptune's Harvest fertilizer above.

Another fertilizer I like to use for my citrus plants is Citrus Tone 5-2-6 which is organic as well. I follow the instructions and apply it three times a year, but then I also use the two fertilizers above as well. Citrus are very heavy feeders!

One of my favorite fertilizers ever, especially for potted outdoor annuals and plants is Osmocote. This is a great product because it can be used for indoor plants or outdoor plants, and it is time-release. The fertilizer itself looks like little balls that you simply mix into the soil, or add to the surface of the soil and gently mix in. It will release fertilizer slowly over the course of a few months and you don't have to remember the last time that you fertilized! I use this product for all my summer potted plants outdoors, but it would be wonderful for indoor houseplants as well.

Lastly, I feel like I can't get away with not mentioning Miracle-Gro which is a great product as well. It is particularly great for foliage plants since it is very high in nitrogen.

FINAL THOUGHTS ON FERTILIZING

Fertilizing is NOT a fix for improper light and poor watering habits.

You should ensure that your houseplants have the appropriate lighting for the variety of plant that you have, and that you are using proper watering techniques and cultural practices FIRST. Once you have these down, then you can focus on fertilizing your plant in order to achieve the best growth that you can in our artificial indoor conditions!

Fertilizing a plant that is in poor light can cause more harm than good.

If you have a flowering houseplant that is not flowering, the reason is likely not enough light. Fertilizing your plant will not cause it to bloom. Moving it to higher light will. The fertilizer will simply enhance the blooming.

I like to take plastic gallon jugs and premix the fertilizer solution ahead of time. This way, I have it ready when I need to use it.

15 REPOTTING

There are many questions that I've been asked when it comes to repotting houseplants:

- How do I know when my houseplant needs repotting?

- How do I know what time of year to repot?

- How exactly DO I repot my plant?

HOW DO I KNOW WHEN MY HOUSEPLANT NEEDS REPOTTING?

There are various ways to tell if your houseplant needs repotting. If you are seeing one or more of the following, it may be time to repot:

- You see a lot of roots coming out of the drainage hole.

- There is no more soil at the surface. Instead, you'll see a hard mat of roots on the surface.

- If you slip the plant out of its pot, the root ball is all in one piece and there doesn't seem to be much soil left.

- Your plant may seem unusually large for its pot. You may also have noticed that it has either stopped growing, or is starting to suffer.

- You may notice that your soil is drying out very quickly despite frequent watering.

- If you can't remember the last time that you repotted your houseplant, it may be time!

- If your plant's leaves have been completely green, and then suddenly many of the tips have turned brown.

WHAT TIME OF YEAR SHOULD I REPOT MY HOUSEPLANT?

The conventional wisdom on repotting is to not do it in the middle of the winter or when the houseplant isn't actively growing. I will go ahead and only partially agree with this. In my opinion, there is nothing wrong with repotting a houseplant in the middle of the winter. It's not ideal, but I've certainly done that if I've felt like it or if it was a potting emergency!

If it's not urgent though, it is better to wait until the plant starts to resume active growth in the springtime. Some people will get scared as if the plant will self-destruct if they repot during the wrong month! Although it certainly is better to repot when a plant is actively growing, you can also repot in the middle of the winter if it is an emergency and your plant is suffering.

HOW TO REPOT A HOUSEPLANT

Finally, here we are! There are many options to think about when you are getting around to repotting your houseplant. What kind of pot should you use? Terra cotta? Plastic pot? Glazed ceramic? What size should the pot be?

STEP 1: CHOOSING A POT

Depending on your plant's growing needs, you need to determine the type of pot to use. If you have a water-loving plant like ferns, it may not be a good idea to plant it in a terra cotta pot. It will dry out much too quickly.

Conversely, if you have a plant that needs to dry out more, it may not be a good idea to plant it in a plastic pot, especially if you go heavy with the watering can. If you tend to "overwater" in general, it may be a good idea to go with terra cotta pots. It all depends on your watering habits, and what your houseplant requires to grow! You could also plant into an inexpensive plastic pot and then slip it into a more decorative pot. It's all personal preference.

As far as size, you typically will want to use just the next size up from where you are. For example, if you have a 4 inch pot, use a 5 inch pot or maybe even a 6 inch pot, but no bigger. The reason is because many plants like to be somewhat pot bound. Also, you don't want to pick a pot so disproportionately large to the root ball that the soil will stay too wet and eventually cause issues, like root rot. See the example below of a Sansevieria that I repotted.

In the picture above, you'll notice I put a piece of broken terra cotta pot to cover the drainage hole. This prevents the soil from escaping when you water. Some people use a mesh at the bottom that serves the same purpose. I have enough broken terra cotta pots in my days that I just reuse these to crock the bottom of my pots.

STEP 2: TAKE YOUR HOUSEPLANT OUT OF ITS OLD POT

Depending on the size and other factors, sometimes the plant will come out of the pot if you gently pull it upwards. If it doesn't come easily out of the pot, I sometimes use a knife to slide around the inside of the pot in order to loosen the root ball.

If there are many matted roots coming out of the drainage hole at the bottom, you may need to just cut those off so that you can slide the plant out of the pot. Don't worry about cutting those roots off, especially if the houseplant is healthy. It will survive and forgive what you did to it. Sometimes, you may want to lean the pot over if it makes it easier to slip the plant out of the pot.

In this repotting example in this chapter, I repotted two Sansevieria. These two cases were much more challenging to take out of the pot, so I wanted to illustrate these for you.

In the photo above, I tried to gently take the Sansevieria out of the pot, but it was so pot bound that I wanted to play it safe and just take a hammer to it! This also created more broken clay pieces to use to cover the drainage holes for new potting jobs.

In the next case below, I had to actually take scissors and cut the plastic pot off of my Sansevieria cylindrica. There was a pup growing out of the drainage hole, so that's why I had to do this. There would have been no other way to safely remove it from the pot.

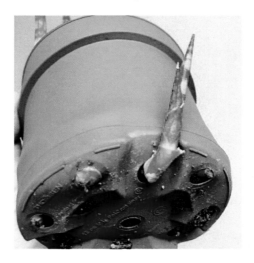

Take a look at the roots once I cut the pot off! Those big, fleshy, beautiful roots!

After you've taken your plant out of the pot, it's a good idea to gently loosen the root ball a little bit. Use both hands and try to pry both the bottom of the root ball, as well as the sides, gently apart. Don't go too crazy. Just loosen the root ball slightly.

If the plant was severely pot bound, loosening the roots a little bit encourages the roots to grow into the soil in the new pot a little more easily. Otherwise they may stay tightly wound even after repotting into the larger pot.

STEP 3: PLACE THE PLANT IN ITS NEW POT

The next thing that I like to do is to place a broken piece of a clay pot at the bottom of the new pot, covering the drainage hole. If you are using new terra cotta pots, I like to completely submerge them in water for half an hour. This will help condition them, otherwise they will wick too much moisture away from your potting mix. They already dry out quickly enough, so you don't need to make the situation worse! I wrote an entire blog post on the pros and cons of terra cotta pots.

After you cover the drainage hole, place a little soil into the bottom of the pot. Then place your plant that you've taken out of the old pot (you should have loosened the root ball already), and place it in the new pot.

You'll want to ensure that you place the plant at about the same depth that it was planted before. Also, you'll want the final soil level to be a little below the top of the actual pot. This is so that when you water, there will be a reservoir and you won't be washing soil away. It will make your watering chores much easier and less messy.

After your plant placement seems correct, it is time to fill the rest of the pot with fresh soil. You can use your hands, a little scoop, or any other creative methods that you can think of. In the photo below, there wasn't much room to work with, so I took a stiff piece of paper (from junkmail!) and used it to guide soil into the pot.

You'll want to gently press any soil down that you place into the pot. The reason is because you want to ensure that the root ball is in firm contact with the soil and that you don't have any air pockets. This will ensure good root growth. Don't pack the soil with all your might though!

In cases where I have more room to work with, unlike the tight working conditions I had in the photo above, I sometimes pre-moisten the soil before I add it to the new pot.

The reason I do this is that sometimes the new soil mix is so dry that it takes a while to wet out adequately. To do this, take some fresh potting soil and place some in a pot that has drainage holes. Then water it and let it soak through until the potting mix is thoroughly moistened. Warm water will tend to work better for this purpose.

Sometimes the water will sit on top for a while and will take a while to penetrate. Once it is pre-moistened though, it'll be much easier to work with, and it'll make watering your plant so much easier because the water will penetrate the soil quickly instead of sitting on the surface for a while. This will ensure that you're giving your newly potted plant a good start in its new pot.

STEP 4: WATER YOUR HOUSEPLANT

After you're done repotting, the last step is to water your plant! By this point in the book, you know I'm going to tell you to water THOROUGHLY.

I will tend to take quite a few of my plants to the sink, give them a thorough watering, let all the water drain away, and then place the plant back in its growing location.

I recommend this watering method even for succulents like Sansevieria and others. Some people may think "oh it's a cactus" or "oh it's a succulent"

and only put a tiny bit of water at a time. If you are doing so, you are doing a disservice to your plant. You may be only getting the top part of the roots wet but not the bottom areas. Even though you "watered it," your plant may appear that it is dehydrating and be dying a slow death because there may be dry pockets of soil.

So give your plant a thorough soaking, let the water drain, and you are done! In most cases, you will then wait until the surface of the soil is dry to the touch before you water again. I cannot emphasize these watering tips enough.

If you can't move the plant to the sink because it is too big or awkward to move, just make sure that the plant does not sit in water in the saucer. You'll want to drain that water away. If you allow a plant to sit in water for extended periods of time, the roots will eventually rot and you will kill the plant. One trick I've used in the past is to use a turkey baster to remove that water for plants that are too big or awkward to move.

16 HUMIDITY

How to increase humidity for your houseplants has been a very misunderstood topic of debate among houseplant growers everywhere! Unless you are growing only cacti and succulents, it is important to understand the topic of humidity and the most effective ways on how to increase humidity for your houseplants.

One point I'd like to make is that even for plants that love humidity, if you are not watering them properly, trying to increase humidity won't do much for you. Proper soil moisture is much more important than having a plant growing in dry soil but with high humidity. If you have proper soil moisture and higher humidity (for plants that like it), then you will be winning.

Let me first talk about the least effective ways to increase humidity, and work our way up from there until I discuss my recommendation for the ultimate way to increase humidity for your plants. Or you could forget about humidity loving plants and only grow cacti and succulents, but that would be a bit boring...

MISTING YOUR HOUSEPLANTS

Are you an obsessive mister? Do you run around from plant to plant and mist your houseplants daily? The only benefit to misting is that you DO get a forearm and hand workout, but that is about it!

Contrary to popular belief, misting is NOT an effective way to increase humidity! It may increase humidity instantaneously, but it is extremely short lived and ineffective. So spare yourself the work! I occasionally do use a mister sometimes, but for purposes other than to increase humidity.

If you are using a mister to wet the leaves of your plants so you can wipe them down to keep them clean, or maybe mist your exposed Phalaenopsis orchid roots so that they stay hydrated, that's fine! But don't expect it to effectively increase your humidity. It just simply does nothing.

In fact, if you overdo it, you can create problems for yourself! Misting your plants at night, coupled with cooler temperatures, is an invitation for fungal diseases. Certain plants like begonias, and many others, are prone to powdery mildew. Misting, especially with cool water, can also cause unsightly blotches on plants like African Violets.

So put that mister down! There are better ways...

PLACING HOUSEPLANTS ON A PEBBLE TRAY

This method is OK! You would simply take a tray of some sort, fill it with pebbles, and add water so that the water level is just under the top of the pebbles. Then simply place your houseplants on top.

As the water evaporates, it will create a little humid microclimate for your plants.

Of course, this has its limitations! It is really only practical if you have smaller plants. And if you have a lot of plants, it simply isn't easy, nor practical, to have trays everywhere around your home! But it is a much better method than misting.

GROUPING PLANTS TOGETHER

Plants naturally release water through a process called transpiration. The more plants you group together, the better it will be! You will be creating a little humid microclimate within your own home.

Of course, if you are a plant hoarder like me, this will happen anyway! But there is the added benefit of extra humidity as well!

PLACE PLANTS IN NATURALLY HUMID AREAS

Do you have any houseplants that need humidity to do their best? Why don't you place them in higher humidity areas of your house? Bathrooms are a perfect choice!

Assuming that you have the appropriate light in a bathroom, why not place your humidity loving plants there if you can to take advantage of humidity created by your daily shower?

USE A HUMIDIFIER

In my opinion, this is the best and easiest way to increase the humidity for your houseplants. Especially if you live in areas with cold winters and forced air heating. My indoor air gets painfully dry in the winter, much to the dismay of my ferns, Calatheas, and other humidity loving plants. Not to mention my poor, dry, flaky skin!

I use a humidifier for my sunroom, mainly in the winter time because of the very dry air, where I have much of my collection concentrated in.

I was tired of the cheap drugstore-type humidifier. They are poorly constructed and have no features. I've learned my lesson. The humidifier I chose is a bit pricier than many, but in the long run, it is the most effective and probably even the cheaper route! I don't want to keep buying a humidifier every year!

I have been absolutely thrilled with the Levoit 6L Hybrid Ultrasonic Humidifier. I absolutely LOVE this humidifier! I have mine placed between our sunroom and our bedroom, so that both plants and people can share in the benefit! My plants will benefit from increased humidity, and so will my skin!

There are many different humidifiers on the market, so do your research and choose one that best suits your needs.

17 THE BEST THING YOU CAN DO FOR YOUR HOUSEPLANTS

Although they're called "houseplants," we seem to forget that these are living beings that evolved over the millennia outdoors. Plants are not meant to be inside, so this chapter is focused on when to put plants outside in Spring, and how to do it.

The "indoors" wasn't even a thing until very recent times in the history of our Earth! That being said, I would wither up and die if I couldn't be surrounded by houseplants in my home and office, but we need to keep in mind that nature does a better job than people ever could.

When houseplants are indoors, we will be the most successful if we keep in mind how the particular plant would grow in nature. However, the absolute best thing that you could do for your houseplants is to move them outdoors during the summer.

WHY YOUR HOUSEPLANT WILL THRIVE OUTSIDE

There are so many reasons that your houseplants will thrive outdoors:

- Rainwater is almost always preferable over tap water. Some plants are sensitive to the additives in tap water. Also, rainwater seems to perform miracles because it contains nitrogen in the form that plants can use, and your houseplant will respond enthusiastically. Rain also will wash away any dust that has accumulated on the leaves while indoors. It's like giving yourself a facial and washing all the schmutz off your face. Except it's not just for the looks. Plants will be able to photosynthesize more efficiently if their leaves are clean.

- The humidity and air circulation outdoors will give your tropical plants what they need to thrive. The air circulation and wind will make the plants sturdier and stronger. Indoor, stale, bone dry air resulting from forced air heating systems wreaks havoc on our poor houseplants.

- The brighter light outdoors will greatly benefit your plant's growth, although you have to be very careful when you first acclimate your plants to the outdoors.

Often times, plants that have never done much for you indoors will take off and grow luxuriantly after a few months outdoors. The Alocasia below slowly was languishing indoors in our sunroom. They just seem to detest the indoors for long periods of time. The light indoors wasn't the issue, but humidity was.

Alocasia plants love high humidity, and unless you have a greenhouse, it is difficult to achieve the conditions that they need. So last summer, I placed this plant outdoors in the shade, and it thrived. It continually threw out leaf after leaf, and each one was bigger than the prior one. Notice how much bigger the leaf in the upper left-hand corner is from the other 2 leaves in the picture. Not only that, this plant actually bloomed for me over the following winter. (The blooms weren't anything spectacular, but an achievement nonetheless!)

I love to summer my orchids outdoors as well. Often times, orchids that have never flowered will suddenly flower for you. I had one orchid burst out with several flowers outdoors and it never put on such a display indoors. Moth orchids and Christmas cactus, among some others, will benefit from being outdoors because a drop in nighttime temperature will help trigger blooming.

HOW TO TRANSITION YOUR HOUSEPLANTS TO GROW OUTSIDE

Unfortunately, it's not as simple as just moving your houseplants outside. Almost, but not quite. There are a couple things that you need to remember when you move your houseplants outside:

- Tropical plants just don't do cold weather. Some of them are surprisingly tolerant though. As a general rule, wait until the nighttime temperatures are at consistently a minimum of 50F (10C). I like to push the limits sometimes, but if you do so, monitor your plant closely. Look for signs of stress. For example, I couldn't resist a great price on a hibiscus plant that I saw once, so I purchased it. I knew it was too early, but I couldn't resist. I noticed that night time temperatures in the 40F-45F range was much too cold for these plants. The leaves were looking a little droopy. To compensate, I moved the plant into the garage each evening until the nights were warm enough to grow in its permanent location outdoors. On the other hand, I had also purchased two huge Boston ferns and they seemed to be perfectly fine to have a few cooler nights. Push the limits and experiment, but keep a close eye on them for signs of stress. If you're in doubt, stick with my original recommendation of minimum night time temperatures of at least 50F.

- When you move your plants outdoors, do NOT put them in the sun, at least initially. Even if your plant grew in a sunny window indoors, the intensity of the light outdoors is much greater. Your plant will need a period of what is called hardening off. So when you take your plant outside, place your plant in COMPLETE shade and let it stay there for a few days before changing location. Then gradually move it to a location with more light, but only if your specific type of plant requires it. If you don't harden your plant off, the leaves will quickly burn.

- Try and place your houseplants in a sheltered area outdoors in an area that is protected from the wind. I've had many plants blow over and have had the pots broken or the plants themselves damaged.

A FEW THINGS TO KEEP IN MIND

- Your houseplant will probably require more frequent watering outdoors. Warmer temperatures and air circulation will dry out the soil much more quickly.

- Make sure you regularly fertilize your plants in the summer because they will be rapidly growing.

- You may want to repot your plants when you move them outside. It's so much easier to perform this task outdoors. Remember that in nature, the soil is constantly replenishing itself with organic matter, so give your plant extra care and repot it every so often, or at least top dress with fresh soil and add fertilizer.

I move as many of my houseplants that I can outside. Of course, I leave a few indoors so that the house doesn't look barren, but your plants will thank and reward you after a nice long summer outdoors!

CONCLUSION

This concludes Essential Houseplants for Beginners! I hope that you have enjoyed reading this book, and I would be eternally grateful if you could leave me a review on Amazon.

I hope this book has given you the knowledge, confidence and enthusiasm to help you demystify houseplant care. Once you realize that houseplant care really isn't that difficult once you understand a few principles, it can become a very fulfilling lifelong hobby!

Finally, please don't forget to visit my houseplant blog site at www.ohiotropics.com where I regularly write various articles on the care of a large variety of houseplants. You can easily subscribe by email as well. I send all my subscribers regular communication emails every time I have a new blog post or have special news to share.

You can also find me on Instagram (@ohiotropics) where I post daily, inspirational and informative houseplant care photos and tips.

Lastly, I have launched a houseplant consultation service where I have helped numerous people over the phone, or by Skype. Read about my houseplant consultation service on my blog. I will help you with anything that you need related to houseplant care.

I wish you the best of luck in your houseplant journey and if you have any questions at all, I am here to help! You can reach me at theohiotropics@gmail.com.

ABOUT THE AUTHOR

Raffaele Di Lallo is the founder of Ohio Tropics and helps tens of thousands of people learn how to grow houseplants through his daily tips on Instagram and his blog site at www.ohiotropics.com. He has a very large and rapidly growing follower base on Instagram and can be found @ohiotropics.

His blog site, www.ohiotropics.com, has rapidly grown in popularity and was named one of the top 25 houseplant blogs on the Internet according to www.feedspot.com. His blog site has readers in over 160 countries and posts primarily about houseplant care.

Besides being a lifetime gardener, he received his Certificate of Home Horticulture from the Oregon State University as a part of their Master Gardener program, completed a Green Gardener program at the Cleveland Botanical Gardens, and is a member of the American Orchid Society. Raffaele earned a B.S. in Chemical Engineering from Northwestern University in Evanston, IL.

Raffaele has been interviewed for multiple podcasts, including On the Ledge, hosted by the venerable Jane Perrone in the U.K. He has also been a guest blogger on numerous sites and has written for www.gardeningknowhow.com and www.unusualseeds.net. His enthusiasm for gardening and houseplants is infectious and has inspired countless individuals both locally and around the world.

Essential Houseplants for Beginners is Raffaele's second book. His first book, Moth Orchid Mastery: The Novice's Guide to Mastering Moth Orchid Culture in Less than 1 Hour, was a #1 New Release on Amazon in many categories. It is available in eBook, paperback, and audio formats. Moth Orchid Mastery is geared to be a practical guide for the complete novice to be able to easily grow and rebloom Phalaenopsis, a plant that has confounded many beginners.

Raffaele prides himself on explaining houseplant care in a very accessible fashion and believes that EVERYONE can develop a "green thumb."

Made in United States
North Haven, CT
18 February 2022

16233382R10055